IS
ES

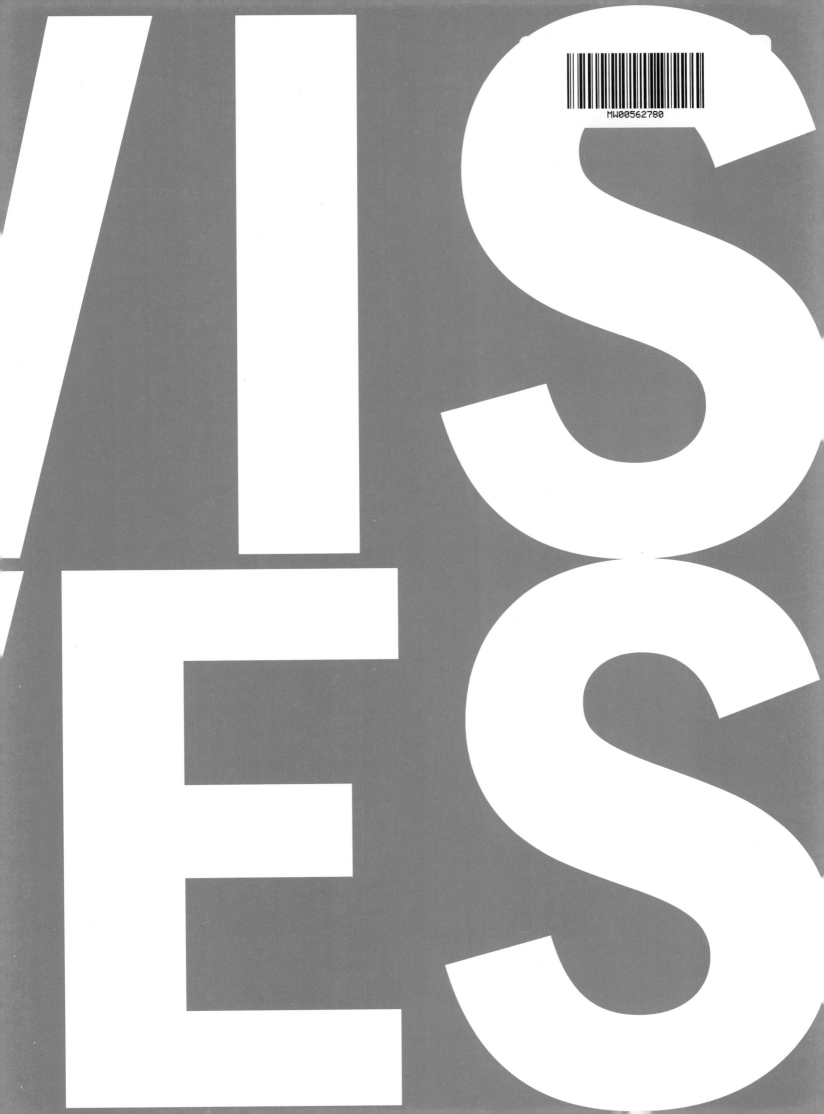

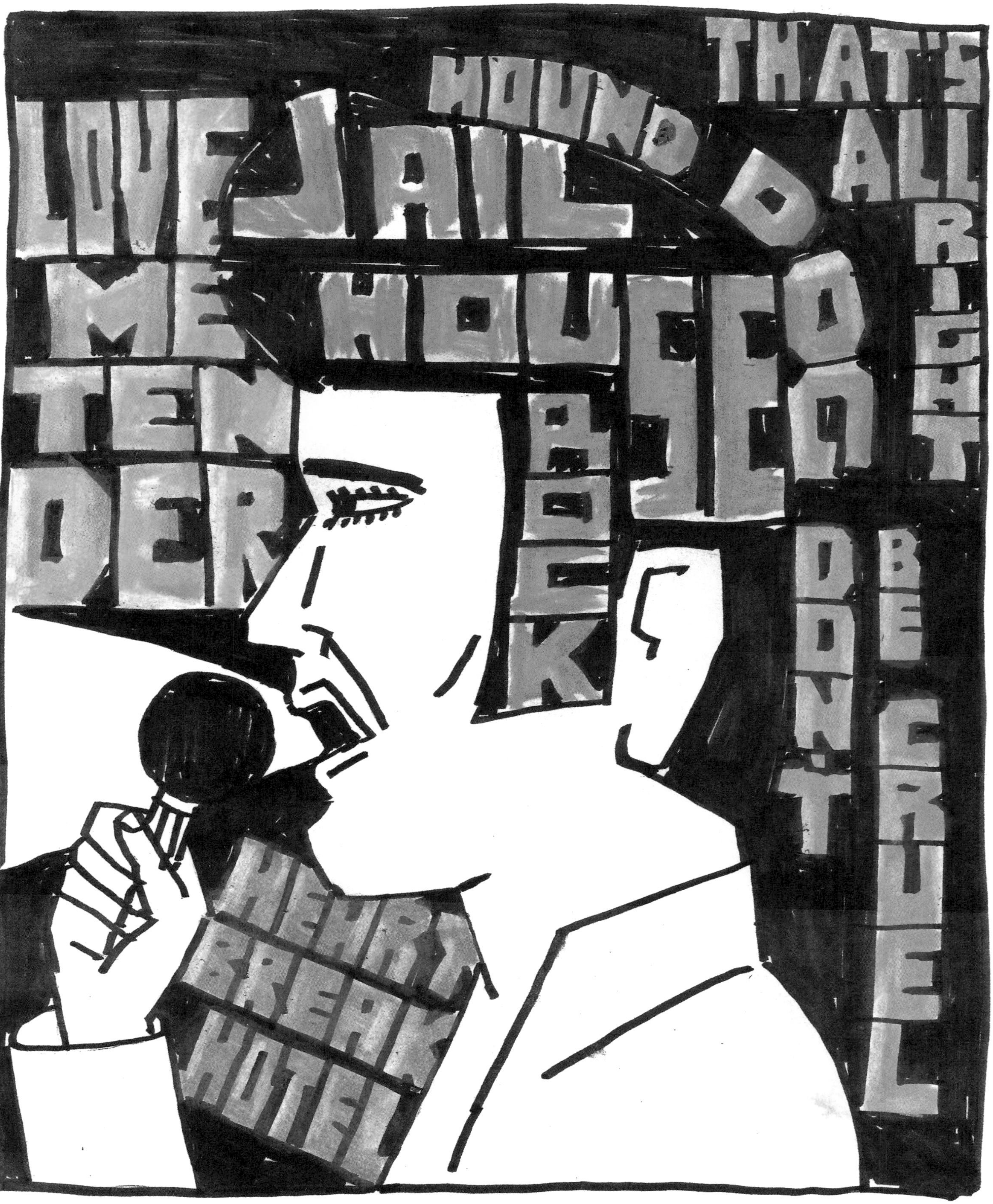
LOVE ME TENDER
HOUND DOG
JAILHOUSE ROCK
THAT'S ALL RIGHT
DON'T BE CRUEL
HEART BREAK HOTEL

The Mighty
ELVIS
A Graphic Biography

Steven Brower
Seymour Chwast

Seymour Chwast

For Paula, from a fool such as I, I want you, I need you, I love you.

Steven Brower

For Kati, who was with me the day Elvis died. And still puts up with me.

ISBN: 978-1-68405-560-9

22 21 20 19 1 2 3 4

Designer and Illustrator: Seymour Chwast
Text: Steven Brower
Associate Designer: Camille Murphy

YoeBooks.com

Yoe Books is a trademark of Gussoni-Yoe Studio, Inc.
Yoe is a registered trademark of Gussoni-Yoe Studio, Inc.

Craig Yoe & Clizia Gussoni, Chief Executive Officers and Creative Directors • Jeff Trexler, Attorney • Steven Thompson, Proofreader and Publicist

IDW Publishing

Chris Ryall, President, Publisher, & CCO • John Barber, Editor-In-Chief • Cara Morrison, Chief Financial Officer • Matt Ruzicka, Chief Accounting Officer • David Hedgecock, Associate Publisher • Jerry Bennington, VP of New Product Development • Lorelei Bunjes, VP of Digital Services • Justin Eisinger, Editorial Director, Graphic Novels & Collections • Eric Moss, Senior Director, Licensing and Business Development

Ted Adams and Robbie Robbins, IDW Founders

November 2019. First printing. IDW Publishing, a division of Idea and Design Works, LLC. Editorial offices: 2765 Truxtun Road San Diego, CA 92106. Printed in Korea.

IDW Publishing does not read or accept unsolicited submissions of ideas, stories, or artwork.

Contents

6   Introduction

8   In the Beginning

10   Sun Records

12   Musical Influences

14   First Records

16   Col. Parker

18   Jackie Gleason

19   Milton Berle

20   Ed Sullivan

22   In the Army

25   Graceland

28   Viva Las Vegas

30   Frank Sinatra

31   Concerts

32   49 Women (and One Man) Who Dated Elvis

33   Pink Cadillac

36   Poster

38   Masculine Idols / Heroes

40   Films

42   Comeback

43   The Beatles

44   Elvis Meets Nixon

46   What He Wore

48   Hair

50   Guitars

52   Songs

54   Tours

56   Priscilla

58   Divorce / Drugs

60   Final Days

62   Filmography

64   Albums

66   Singles

68   The Critics

70   Elvis Speaks

72   What He Ate

72   Bibliography

Elvis Lives!

Elvis Presley was one of the most important cultural figures of the second half of the 20th century. Arguably greater than Frank Sinatra, who came immediately before, and The Beatles, and Bob Dylan, immediately after, he changed the course of music going forward and fanned the flames of a split between the generations.

Even greater than the music, there was the look. Elvis appeared to walk straight out of the film, *The Wild One*, starring Marlon Brando and Lee Marvin and embodied Brando's anarchistic rebellious attitude, his loner identity, as well as his sensuous good looks. Around the edges of the status quo something was brewing. Following WWII, rebellion seemed to be in the air. A rift began to form between the fathers who served and the children for whom they had fought, disturbing the relative post-war calm. The Beat Generation of Jack Kerouac, Neil Cassady, and Allen Ginsberg in literature, Jackson Pollock and abstract expressionists in the art world, and Brando and James Dean in television and film, heralded a new societal attitude. It was through this culturally cracked lens that Elvis strode.

Was Elvis the "King of Rock 'n' Roll" as he is commonly referred to? An exact definition of Rock and Roll does not exist. Is it simply a combination of the Blues, Gospel, Boogie-Woogie, Jazz, Country, and Rhythm and Blues? Or is it, in its origins, only when a Caucasian performs African American music? If the former, then certainly contemporaries Chuck Berry and Little Richard should qualify for that honor, as they wrote their own songs. If the latter, Presley was not the first. Bill Haley's first hit, "Crazy, Man Crazy," and subsequent single "Shake, Rattle and Roll," preceded Elvis' first recordings by several months and Presley's first national hit by a few years. But while Haley had the sound, he did not have the look. At 28 years of age he appeared old to teens of the day, slightly overweight and balding, with his plaid sports jacket, he resembled a traveling salesman infinitely more than youthful rebellious threat. In contrast, like his audience, Elvis was still in his teens when his first record, "That's All Right," was released.

Elvis had something else to offer: sensuality. With his doleful eyes, dyed jet black hair, and swiveling hips, he could elicit fainting spells and screams from female audience members not seen since the days of Sinatra at the Paramount. Mockingly dubbed "Elvis the Pelvis," he soon appeared on all three television networks, sometimes shot only from the waist up, a first. And there was something else, something the film critic for the British magazine *Sight and Sound* Peter John Dyer in 1959 described, that Elvis' on-screen persona was "aggressively bisexual in appeal."

He never wrote a song. He did not have the four octave range of Roy Orbison, the fevered exuberance of Jerry Lee Lewis, the ecstatic holler of Little Richard, or the guitar chops of Chuck Berry. And yet there was a sensitivity underneath the defiant stance, conveyed through his choice of songs, such as "Love Me Tender," "Don't Be Cruel," "(Let Me Be Your) Teddy Bear," "I Want You, I Need You, I Love You," and "Heartbreak Hotel." He also was exceedingly polite, as Ed Sullivan would declare to a national audience, "I wanted to say to Elvis Presley and the country that this is a real decent, fine boy, and wherever you go, Elvis, … we want to say we've never had a pleasanter experience on our show with a big name than we've had with you…So now let's have a tremendous hand for a very nice person!"

6

Perhaps not the thing his young audience wished to hear in 1956, but it had no negative effect on his career, as the hits kept coming. That same year he made his film debut in the Western, "Love Me Tender" and the future looked promising. The following year he acted in another two, "Loving You" and "Jailhouse Rock," with its classic dance scene choreographed by Elvis. In 1958 he repeated his screen success with "King Creole."

However, a decline was looming that came in two forms. One, the films themselves became increasingly formulaic, one or two per year for a solid decade, beginning in 1960. Many fault his manager, "Colonel" Tom Parker, and Elvis grew increasingly indifferent and bored. The other was being drafted into the army in 1958. While he and RCA, his record company, had the foresight to pre-record a number of songs to be released in his absence, some of which became his greatest hits, he disappeared from the public's view. While he was only gone a mere two years, his presence never seemed quite the same. And the times they were a'changing. With the folk movement and blues revival in the U.S. and the explosion in Britain led by the Beatles and the Rolling Stones, the world, music, and Elvis would never be quite the same. This, combined with the burgeoning Vietnam War and Elvis was rendered something that only a few years prior seemed impossible: passé.

And while this new generation of rockers, from Dylan to all four Beatles, acknowledged their debt, Elvis, the celebrity, seemed to retreat inside Graceland with his much younger bride, Priscilla, his Cadillacs, and his Memphis Mafia. He had a hit in 1963 with the halfhearted "Devil in Disguise." Asked what he thought of the recording, John Lennon declared the song "a miss" and that Elvis sounded "like Bing Crosby now."

His comeback came five years later, in 1968, with his NBC special *Singer Presents...ELVIS*. The highlight of that special was Elvis sitting down with his original Sun Records band, recalling his halcyon rockabilly days. The show was a ratings success and his career received a much-needed jolt but it was obvious from his short haired, clean-shaven, sharp dressed look that he couldn't be placed further from the current music scene of Cream, Jimi Hendrix, and The Grateful Dead, et al. Elvis was now and forever an adult.

Cementing his new grown-up image was his bizarre meeting with Richard Nixon in 1970, asking the conservative President for a Bureau of Narcotics and Dangerous Drugs badge and declaring his disdain for the counter-culture. One could not get more establishment than that. After that meeting, Elvis barely resembled his youthful self, with weight gain, tales of shooting out televisions, rumored drug addiction, increasingly odd performances, wavering voice, a much publicized divorce, and declining health. Still, his audience remained loyal, attending his concerts, throwing their panties on stage, and buying his records, over-produced as they were.

It's hard to believe that when Elvis finally "left the building" on August 16, 1977, he was only 42 years old. He has been gone almost as long as he lived. And yet, he has remained indelible on the American psyche, with numerous film portrayals, imitators galore and the occasional sightings. Ever the "King," now and forever, Elvis lives!

—*Steven Brower*

In the Beginning

TENNESSEE
ARKANSAS
Memphis
MISSISSIPPI RIVER
22
MOVING
Oxford
Tupelo
MISSISSIPPI
ALABAMA
Jackson

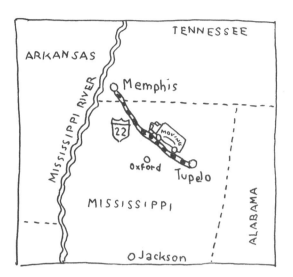

Elvis Aaron Presley was born on January 8, 1935 in Tupelo, Mississippi to Vernon and Gladys. His identical twin brother Jesse Garon Presley was stillborn. Vernon was often unemployed and worked as a milkman, carpenter, farm hand, and truck driver. He built the two-room "shotgun" house where Elvis grew up. In April of the following year, the family survived the Tupelo–Gainesville tornado outbreak.

In 1938 the family lost their home after Vernon was found guilty of check fraud. He was jailed for eight months at Parchman Farm (Mississippi State Penitentiary). As a result, Gladys and Elvis moved in with relatives. In September of 1941, Elvis entered the first grade at East Tupelo Consolidated. Elvis, who was shy and wore glasses, was seen as an average student by his teachers. The family attended the Pentecostal Assembly of God church, where Elvis heard gospel music.

In 1946 Presley entered a new school in Milam, for the sixth grade; the other kids saw him as a loner. He brought his guitar to school on a daily basis and was teased as a "trashy" kid who played hillbilly music. After graduating from secondary school, Presley auditioned for the local gospel group, the Songfellows, but was turned down.

For his first job, he worked on an assembly line but quit after a few weeks and became an apprentice electrician at Crown Electric.

On November 6, 1948, Vernon, Gladys, and Elvis moved from Tupelo, Mississippi to Memphis, Tennessee. The following September they moved to Lauderdale Courts, a public housing project. They lived two blocks away from the Ellis Auditorium, where Elvis went to rhythm and blues and gospel concerts.

Elvis attended L. C. Humes High School, where he received a C in music. His music teacher informed him that he did not have an aptitude for singing. He was usually too shy to perform, and was bullied by classmates as a "mama's boy."

By 1950 he began playing in a band with the brothers Dorsey and Johnny Burnette. He got a job ushering at Loew's State Theater. In his junior year he grew out his sideburns and styled his hair with rose oil and Vaseline. By his senior year, he wore flashy clothes. He competes in Humes's annual "Minstrel" show in April 1953, performing "Till I Waltz Again with You," a recent hit for Teresa Brewer. After that, his popularity at school improved greatly.

Elvis listened to WDIA-AM, which played "race records": spirituals, blues, and rhythm and blues. He attended the monthly "All-Night Singings" downtown, where white gospel groups performed music that reflected the influence of African-American spiritual music. Elvis graduated high school in June 1953.

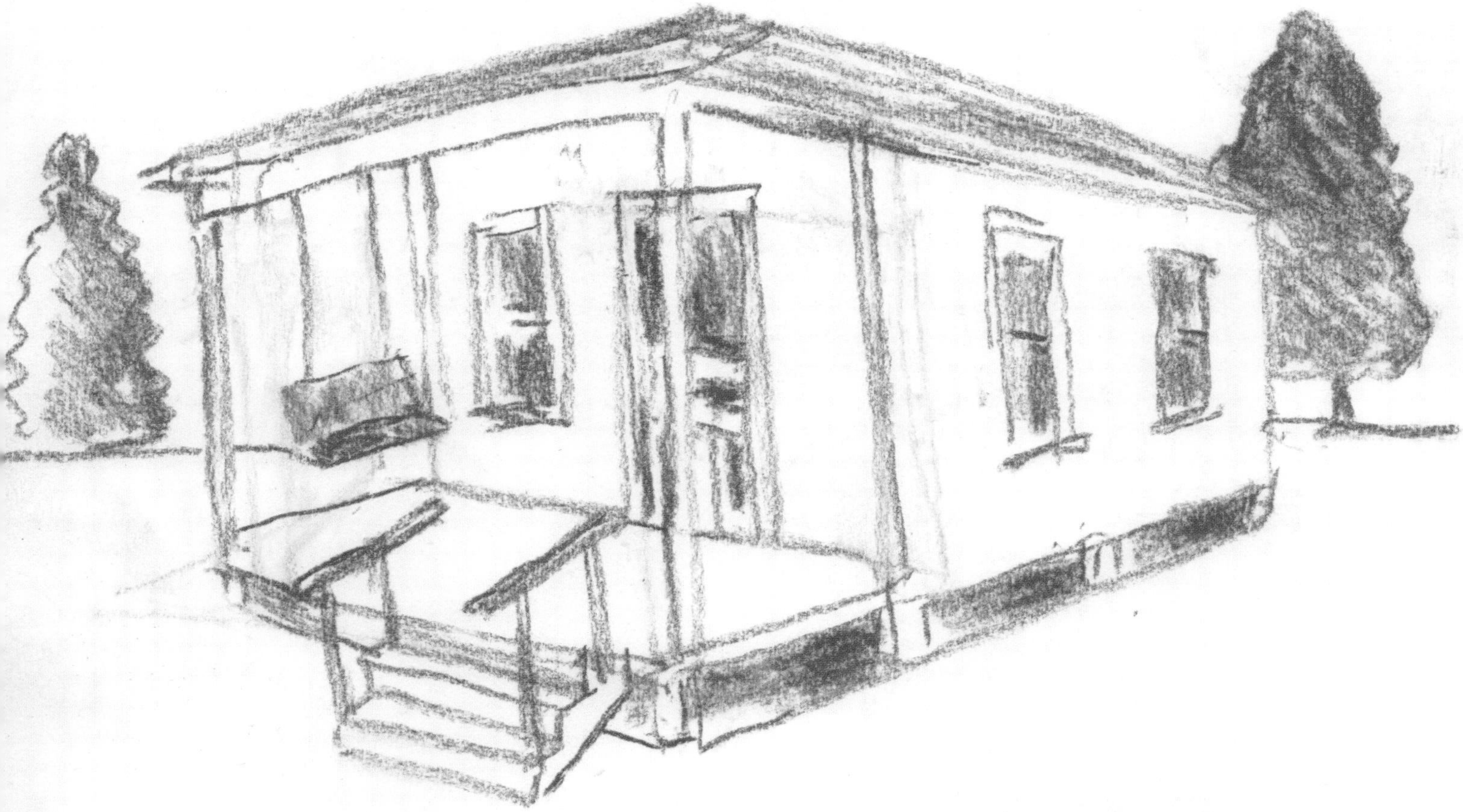

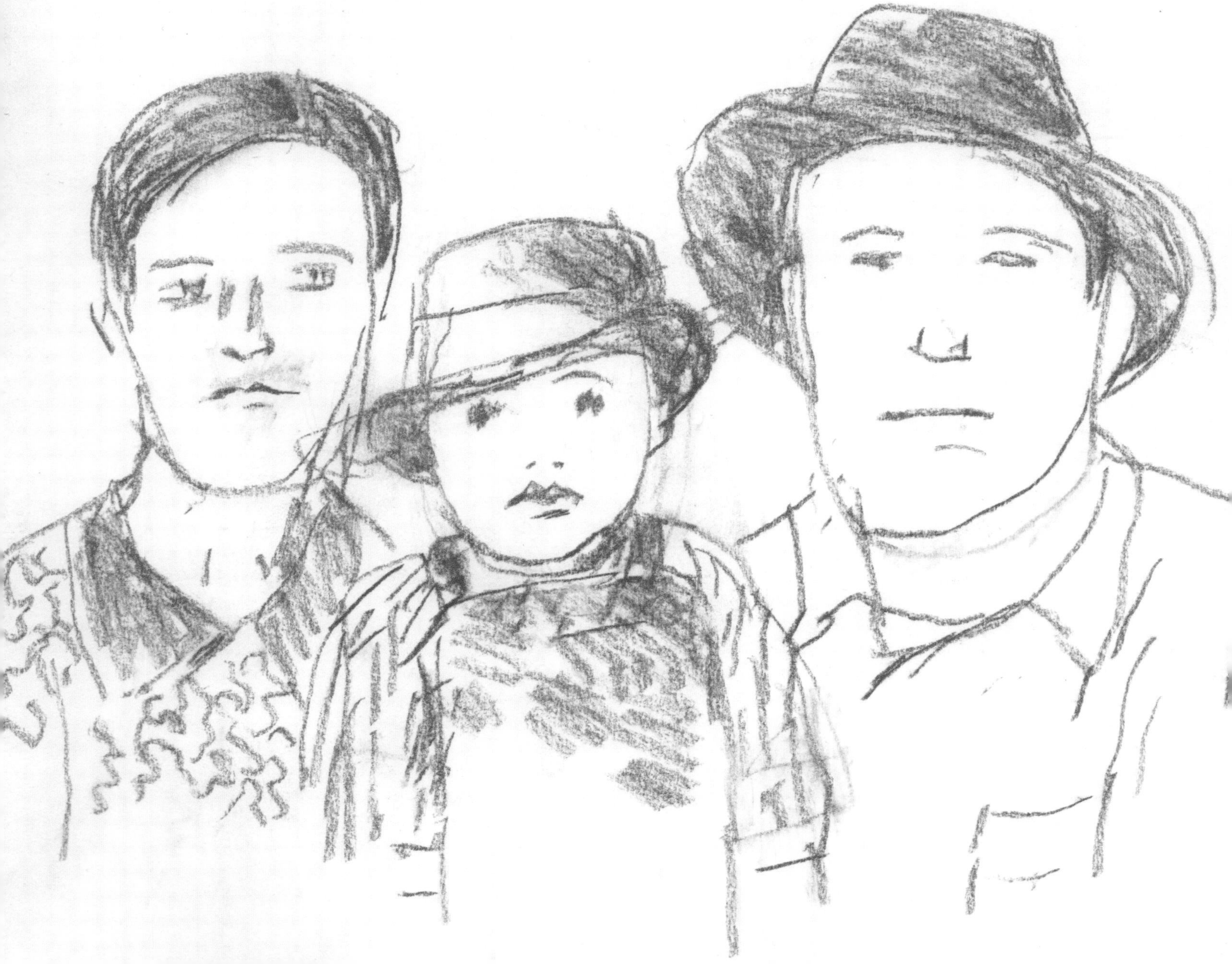

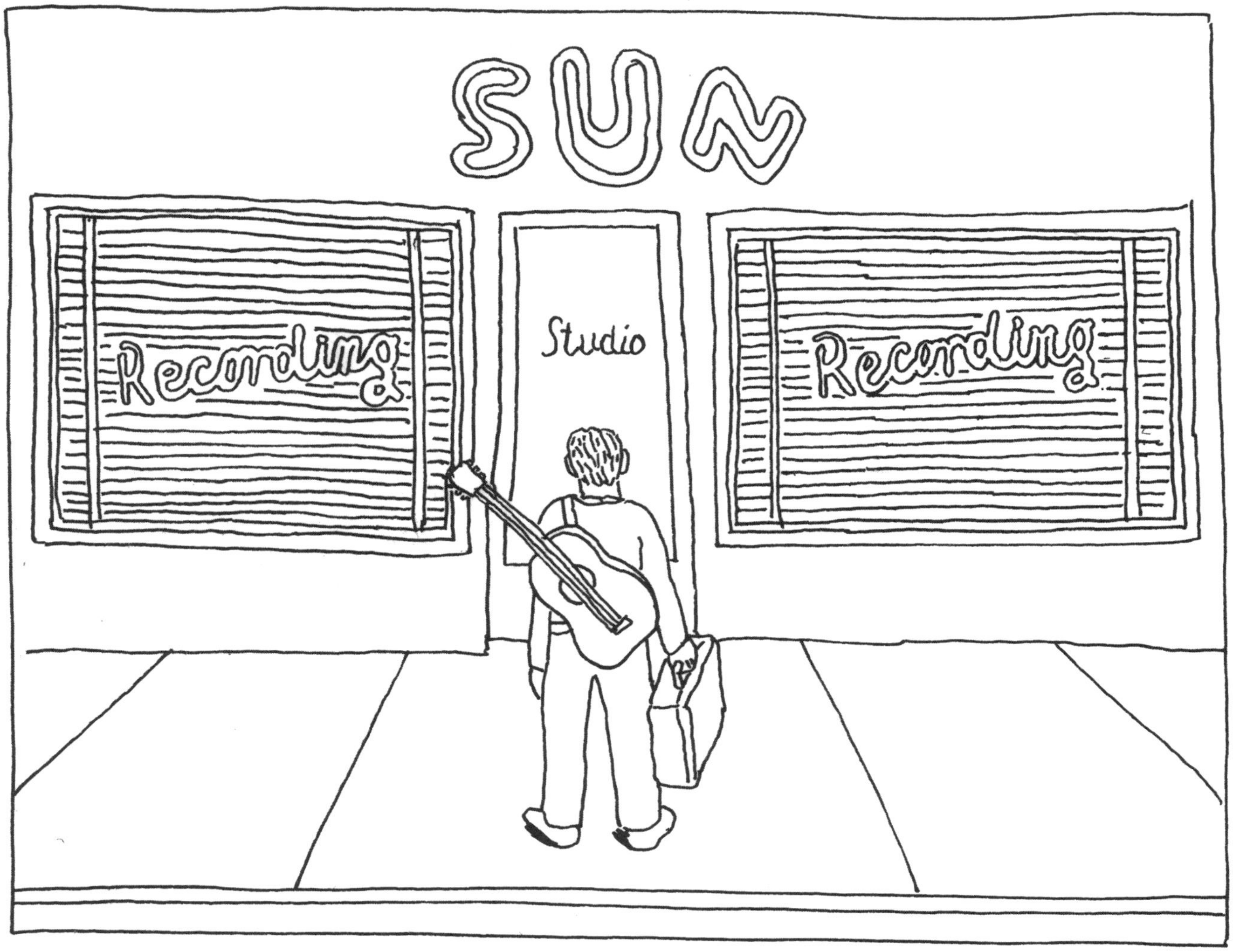
SUN
Recording
Studio
Recording

In August 1953 an 18-year-old Presley walked into the offices of the local Sun Records and paid to record a two-sided acetate disc as a gift for his mother. When asked by receptionist Marion Keisker what kind of singer he was, he said, "I sing all kinds." When she pressed him on who he sounds like, he replied, "I don't sound like nobody." The next January he cut a second acetate at Sun. Sun's owner, record producer Sam Phillips, liked what he heard.

In July, Elvis received a call from local guitarist Scotty Moore and bass player Bill Black, to meet them at Memphis Recording Service for a session with Phillips. After playing songs that did not spark Sam's interest, Elvis played Arthur "Big Boy" Crudup's "That's All Right." It is released as his first single, with Bill Monroe's "Blue Moon of Kentucky" as the B-side. Philips took the demo to local WHBQ radio D.J. "Daddy-O" Dewey Phillips (no relation) who played the demo on the air. The switchboard instantly lit up. By the end of the month, Elvis, Scotty, and Bill performed at the Overton Park Shell in Memphis and the crowd went wild. In October the trio performed at *The Louisiana Hayride*.

On December 4, 1956, an impromptu recording session with Presley and three other Sun artists, Jerry Lee Lewis, Carl Perkins, and Johnny Cash, began at Sun, which Phillips recorded. This recording became known as the "Million Dollar Quartet" but would not be released for 25 years. Cash would later recall, "The first time I saw Elvis, singing from a flatbed truck at a Katz drugstore opening on Lamar Avenue, two or three hundred people, mostly teenage girls, had come out to see him. With just one single to his credit, he sang those two songs over and over. That's the first time I met him."

Sun Records

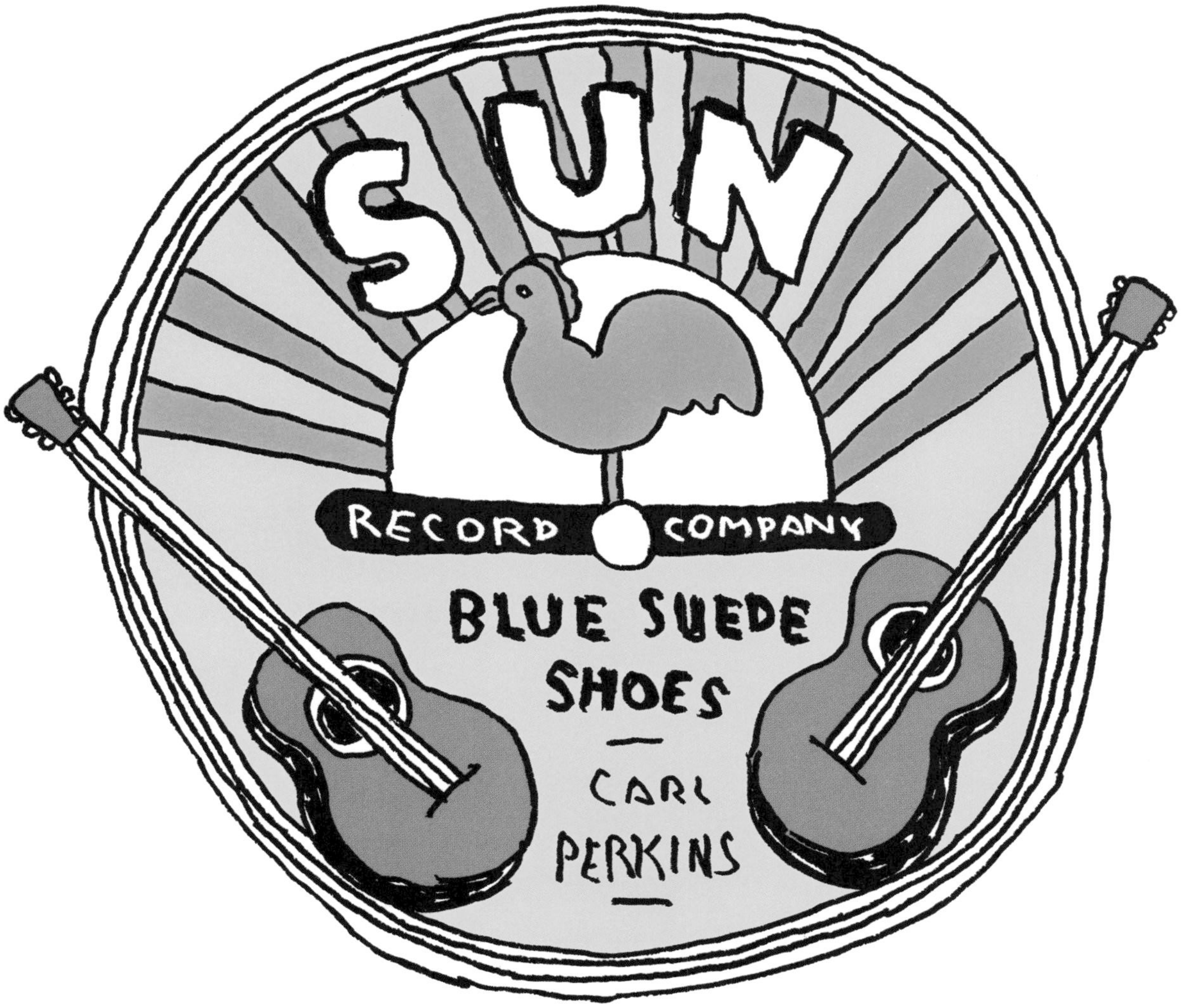
SUN
RECORD COMPANY
BLUE SUEDE SHOES
CARL PERKINS

Jerry Lee Lewis Carl Perkins Johnny Cash Elvis Presley

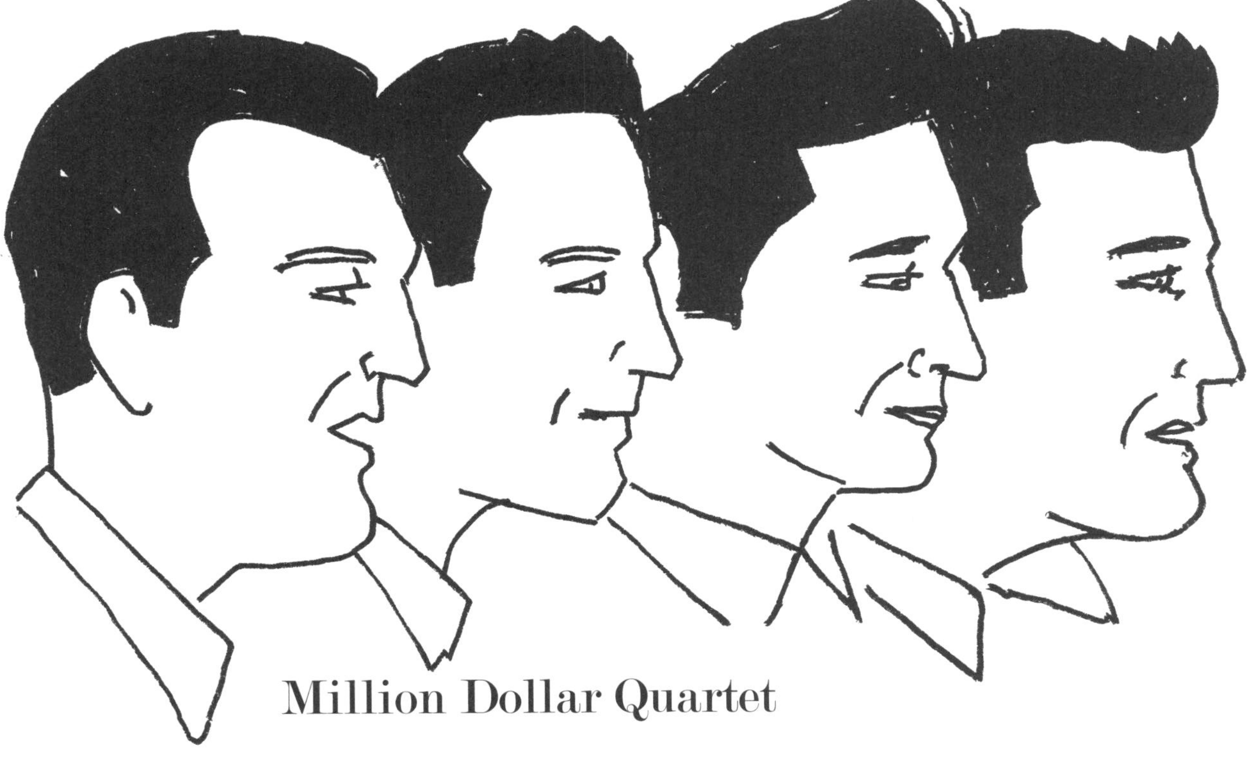

Million Dollar Quartet

Musical Influences

Elvis Presley
and B.B. King

Teresa Brewer

Jake Hess

Bing Crosby

"Big Mama" Thornton

Presley found his earliest musical inspiration close to home. Growing up in Tupelo, he attended the First Assembly of God Church with Vernon and Gladys, where they sang in the choir. Every Saturday night the family gathered around the radio to listen to the day's top country stars on "the Grand Ole Opry."

At age 10 a bespectacled Elvis performed Red Foley's country hit "Old Shep," without accompaniment, at a talent show. The contest, held at the Mississippi-Alabama Fair and Dairy Show was his first public performance. He had to stand on a chair to reach the microphone. Varying accounts have him coming in at second or fifth place. The following year he was given a guitar for his 11th birthday. He had hoped for something else—either a bicycle or a rifle. Taught to play by his Uncle Vester, Vernon's brother, he soon began singing and playing in church.

One of Elvis' elementary school classmates, James Ausborn was the younger brother of local radio star Mississippi Slim (Carvel Lee Ausborn). On the WELO *Saturday Jamboree*, a popular radio talent show broadcast from the local courthouse, Slim combined country music with comedy, and invited the young Elvis to perform. Slim backed Elvis on guitar and taught him new chords and songs. Slim was also good friends with singing cowboy Tex Ritter, who would become another early influence on the impressionable Elvis.

The family moved to Memphis where Elvis attended junior high and then high school. They would gather around the radio to listen to country acts like Eddy Arnold, Sleepy Eyed John, and the Louvin Brothers; and gospel groups like the Blackwood Brothers and the Statesmen (led by Jake Hess).

In the 10th grade Elvis became friends with the brothers Dorsey and Johnny Burnette, who would go on to become rockabilly stars in their own right. They formed a band and Elvis sang backup harmonies. In contrast to their pioneering sound, at parties Elvis would play guitar and croon pop numbers by Dean Martin, Bing Crosby, and Perry Como. He attended all-night gospel singing sessions with his parents at the Ellis Auditorium. Just before he graduated, Elvis performed in the school's annual "Minstrel Show," singing Teresa Brewer's "Till I Waltz Again with You."

Since he could not read music, Presley had to play by ear. He learned all of Hank Snow's songs and cherished

Mississippi Slim

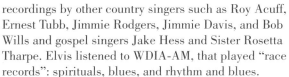

Ray Charles

recordings by other country singers such as Roy Acuff, Ernest Tubb, Jimmie Rodgers, Jimmie Davis, and Bob Wills and gospel singers Jake Hess and Sister Rosetta Tharpe. Elvis listened to WDIA-AM, that played "race records": spirituals, blues, and rhythm and blues.

Later that year he recorded "My Happiness" and the Ink Spots' "That's When Your Heartaches Begin," as a present for his mother at Sun Records, the home of recording artists Rufus Thomas and Junior Parker. He returned to record the traditional folk song "Careless Love," and a country song, "I'll Never Stand in Your Way," a hit that year by Joni James. These recordings caught the attention of Sun owner Sam Phillips who set up a session with Elvis and musicians Scotty Moore on guitar and Bill Black on bass. They recorded Arthur "Big Boy" Crudup's blues song, "That's All Right," with the flip side "Blue Moon of Kentucky," written by Bill Monroe and the Bluegrass Boys. They followed this with many others, including "Good Rockin' Tonight," by Wynonie Harris and "I Don't Care If the Sun Don't Shine," which had been a hit for Dean Martin just prior. For "Baby Let's Play House," by Arthur Gunter, Elvis changed the lyric "You may have religion" to "You may drive a pink Cadillac." Elvis had his first regional hit records in 1954.

At the studio he met blues artist B. B. King, who would later recall, "I remember Elvis as a young man hanging around the Sun Studios. Even then, I knew this kid had a tremendous talent. He was a dynamic young boy. His phraseology, his way of looking at a song, was as unique as Sinatra's. I was a tremendous fan and had Elvis lived there would have been no end to his inventiveness."

Two years later he moved to RCA Records and had hits with "Hound Dog," written by Jerry Leiber and Mike Stoller, originally recorded by Willie Mae "Big Mama" Thornton, and songs originally covered by Little Richard ("Tutti Frutti"), Ray Charles ("I Got A Woman"), and Big Joe Turner ("Shake, Rattle and Roll").

As much as he was influenced, Elvis went on to influence those who came after. According to Bob Dylan, "Hearing him for the first time was like busting out of jail." Likewise, John Lennon stated, "Nothing really affected me until I heard Elvis. If there hadn't been an Elvis, there wouldn't have been a Beatles."

Bill Monroe

Tex Ritter

Johnny Burnette

Little Richard

First Records

Despite all his critics, Elvis was a sudden success. He had his first regional hit with "That's All Right" and after moving to RCA two years later, had his first Billboard number one record with "Heartbreak Hotel." For the next several years the hits kept coming: "I Want You, I Need You, I Love You," "Don't Be Cruel," "Hound Dog," "Love Me Tender," "Too Much," "All Shook Up," "(Let Me Be Your) Teddy Bear," "Jailhouse Rock," "Don't" and "Hard Headed Woman," all reached the top of the charts. He would have several more hits during his army stint that he had prerecorded.

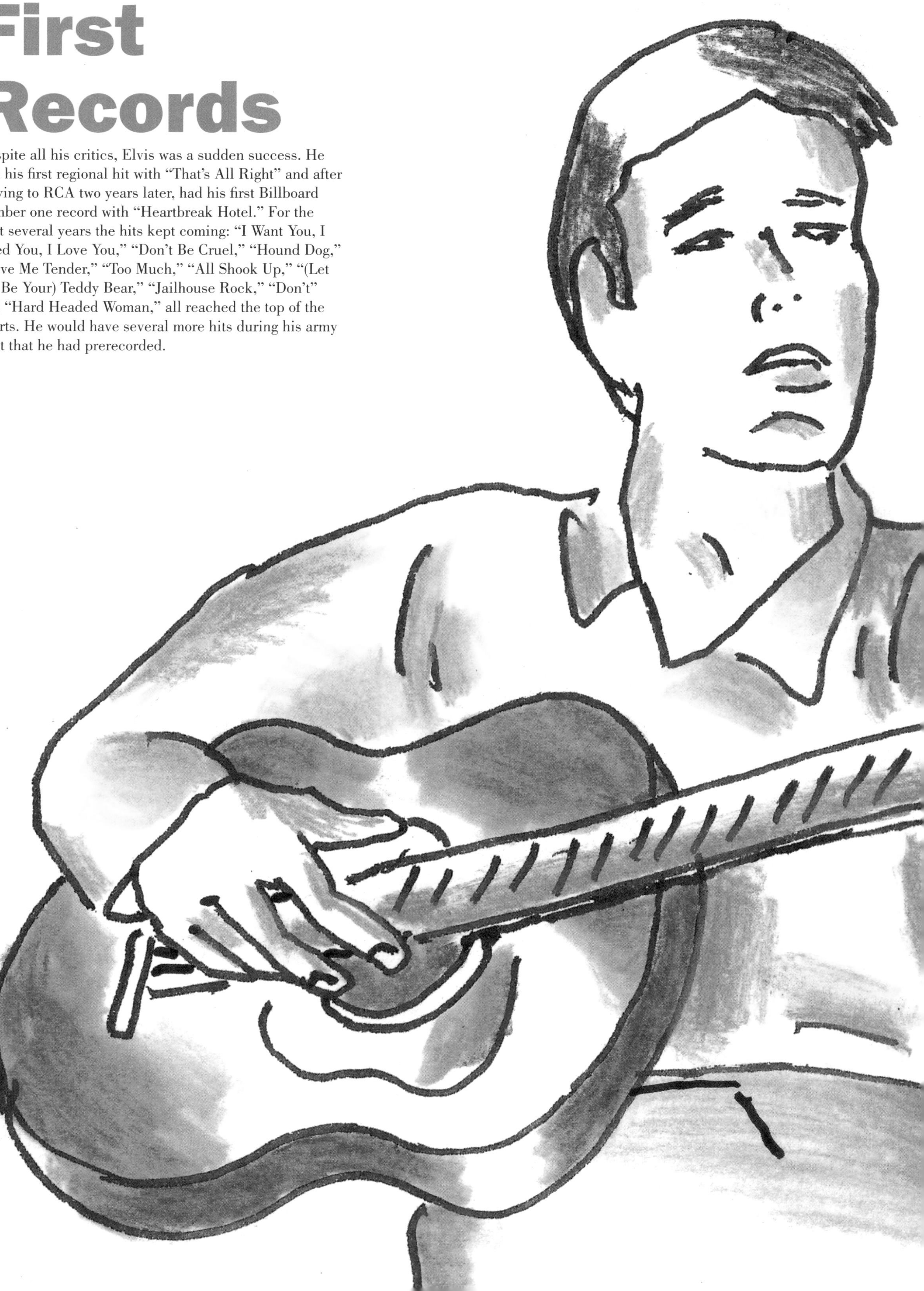

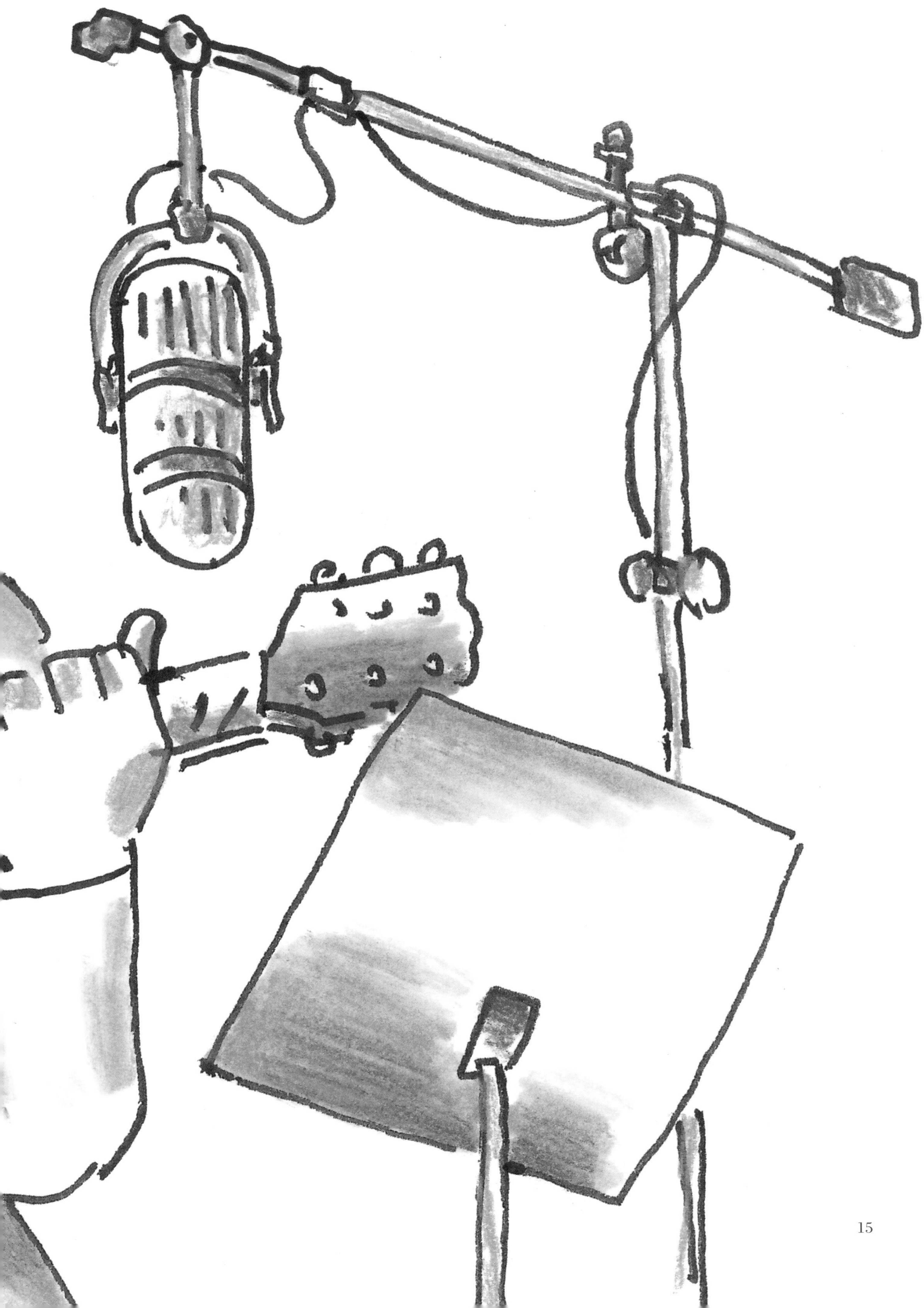

Col. Parker

Andreas Cornelis van Kuijk was born on June 26, 1909 in the Netherlands. As a boy, he worked as a barker at carnivals in his hometown of Breda. At age 15, he moved to the port town of Rotterdam where he worked on boats. It was there that he first developed his wanderlust, wanting to run away to America to make his fortune. He became a person of interest in a murder in Breda and at age 18 he entered the U.S. illegally, when he jumped ship from a Dutch vessel he'd been working on.

He found work at carnivals and enlisted in the United States Army, taking the name "Tom Parker" to disguise that he was an illegal immigrant. He served two years and shortly afterwards re-enlisted. During his second stint, he went AWOL and was charged with desertion. He was put into solitary confinement, which resulted in a mental breakdown. He spent two months in a psychiatric hospital, following which he was discharged from the Army.

In 1935 Parker married and worked at a number of jobs including food concessions and gaming carnivals, and also running "short cons" to survive the Great Depression on as little as $1 a week. In 1938 Parker first became a music promoter for popular singer Gene Austin. By 1945 he was representing country star Eddy Arnold. In 1948 the honorary title "Colonel" was bestowed upon Parker by Louisiana Governor Jimmie Davis in return for working on his election campaign.

In 1955 "Colonel" Tom Parker, who also represented singers Hank Snow and Tommy Sands, became Elvis' exclusive manager for 25% of the profits. Elvis' father had to sign the contract with Parker on his behalf, as he was still a minor. Parker struck a deal with Sun Records owner Sam Phillips to release Elvis from their contract for an unheard of $40,000 and brought Elvis to RCA Records, where he had his first number one national hit, "Heartbreak Hotel," in 1956. That same year he booked Elvis on the Milton Berle and Ed Sullivan shows, and others, making him the highest-paid star on television. Parker sold the merchandising rights to Elvis products, including charm bracelets and record players, earning $22 million by the end of 1956.

Parker arranged a screen test for Elvis with Paramount Pictures, leading to a seven-picture contract. "Love Me Tender," the song from the film of the same name, sold over one million copies in advance sales. Elvis became one of the highest paid, internationally known stars in the world. Elvis starred in as many as two films per year throughout the 1960s. By 1967 Elvis' contract with Parker gave him 50 percent of most of the singer's earnings, including recordings, films, and merchandise. Presley said of Parker, "I don't think I'd have ever been very big if it wasn't for him. He's a very smart man."

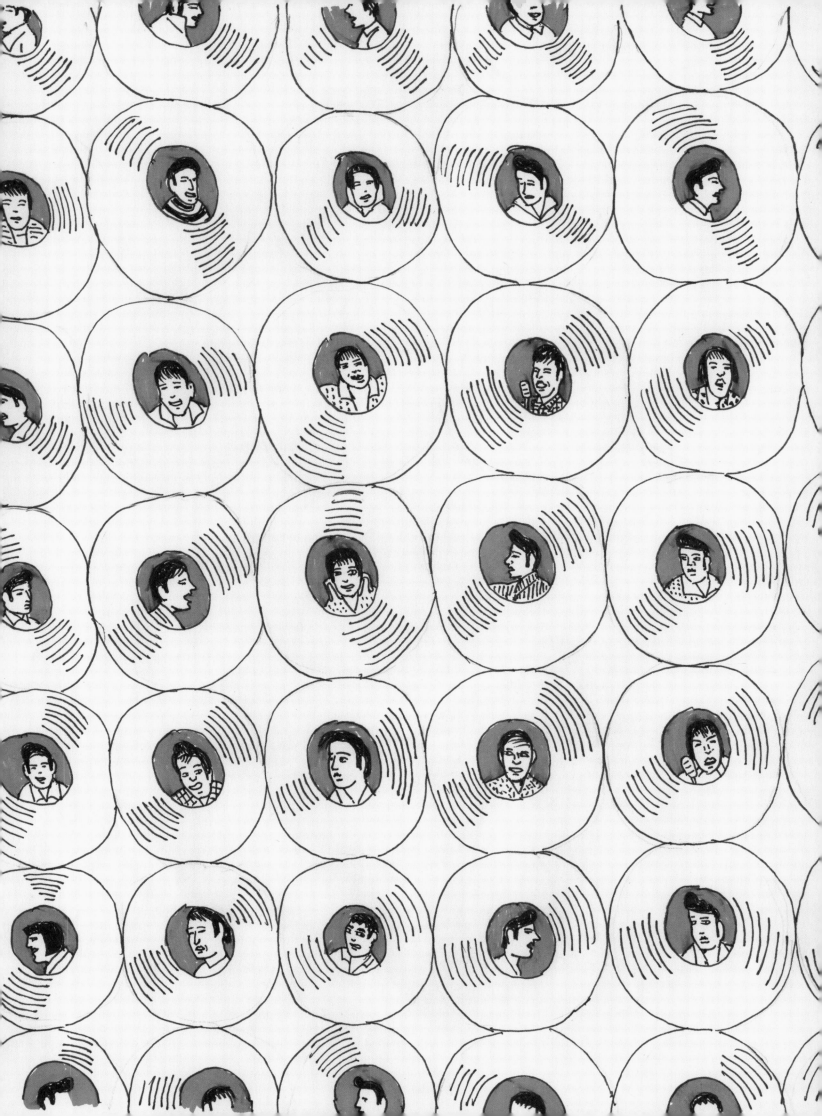

Jackie Gleason

By early January 1956, Elvis was a Billboard number one recording artist. On January 26 he made his first national television appearance on the Jackie Gleason produced *Stage Show* hosted by Jimmy and Tommy Dorsey on CBS. Elvis performed "Shake, Rattle and Roll" and "I Got A Woman."

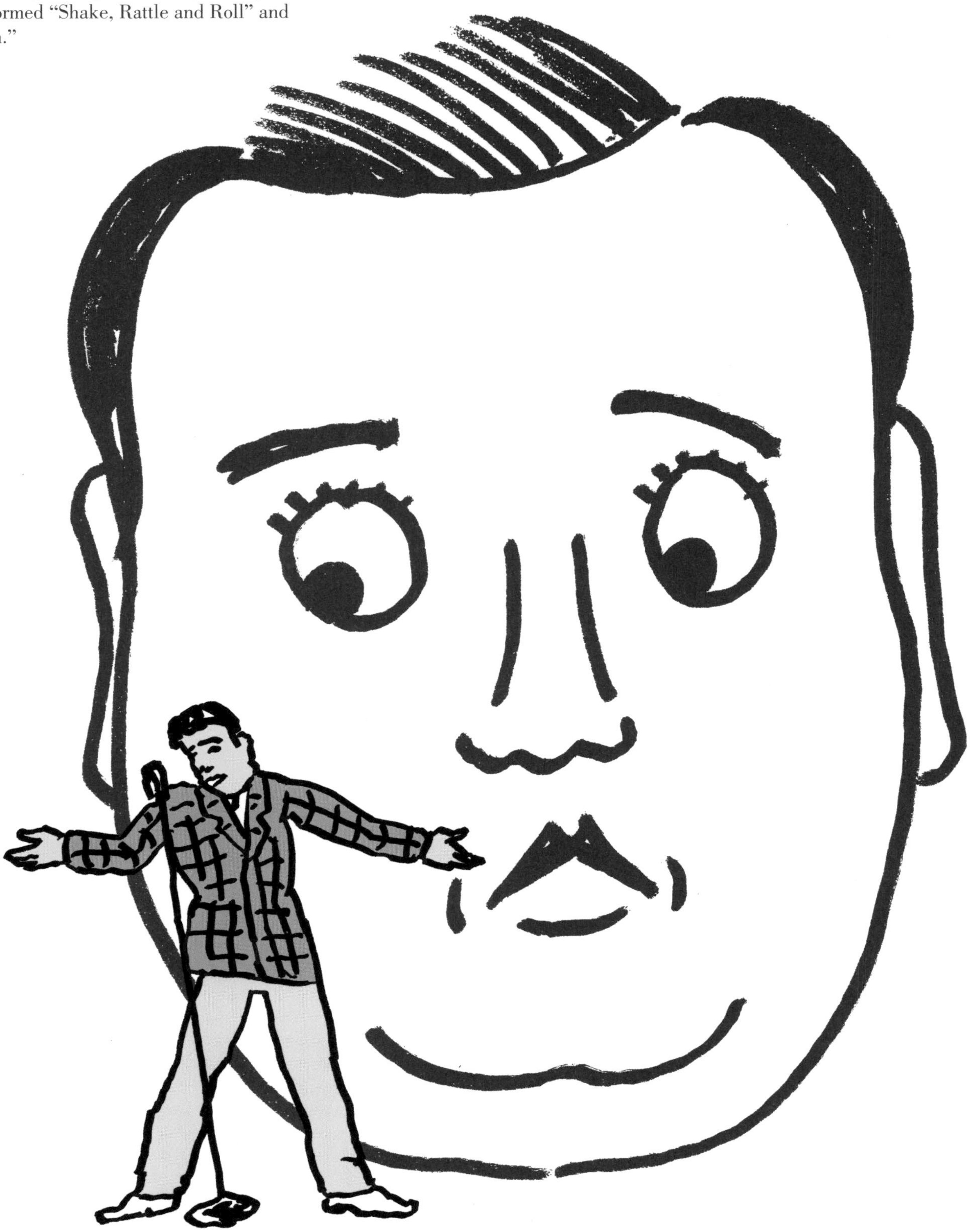

Milton Berle

This is followed in April with the first of two appearances on NBC's *Texaco Star Theatre* starring Milton Berle. The audience went wild. There was a backlash from conservative groups who viewed his moves as vulgar and dangerous to youth. In June Elvis appears on *The Steve Allen Show* in a tuxedo and sings "Hound Dog" to a basset hound, sans guitar.

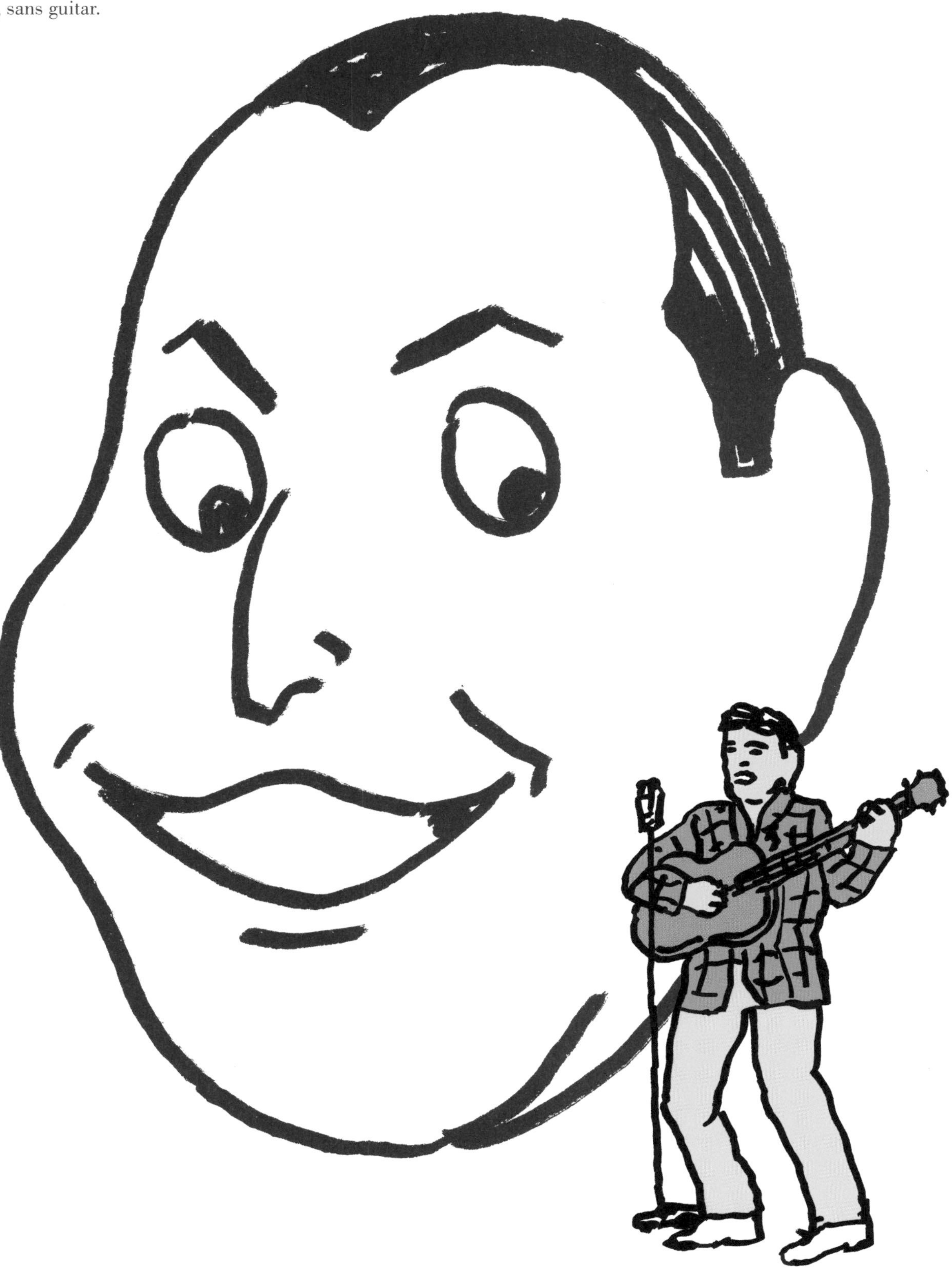

Ed Sullivan

Ed Sullivan, host of *Toast of the Town*, takes notice. Initially reluctant to book him, Elvis makes his first appearance in September of that year. There is an outcry from various religious groups and by his third appearance Presley is shown only from the waist up. Privately Sullivan had conjectured that Presley "got some kind of device hanging down below the crotch of his pants–so when he moves his legs back and forth you can see the outline of his cock...I think it's a Coke bottle...We just can't have this on a Sunday night. This is a family show!"

Actor Charles Laughton hosted the first show, filling in for Sullivan, who was recuperating from a car accident. Elvis is paid $50,000 for three performances. The first show was seen by approximately 60 million viewers.

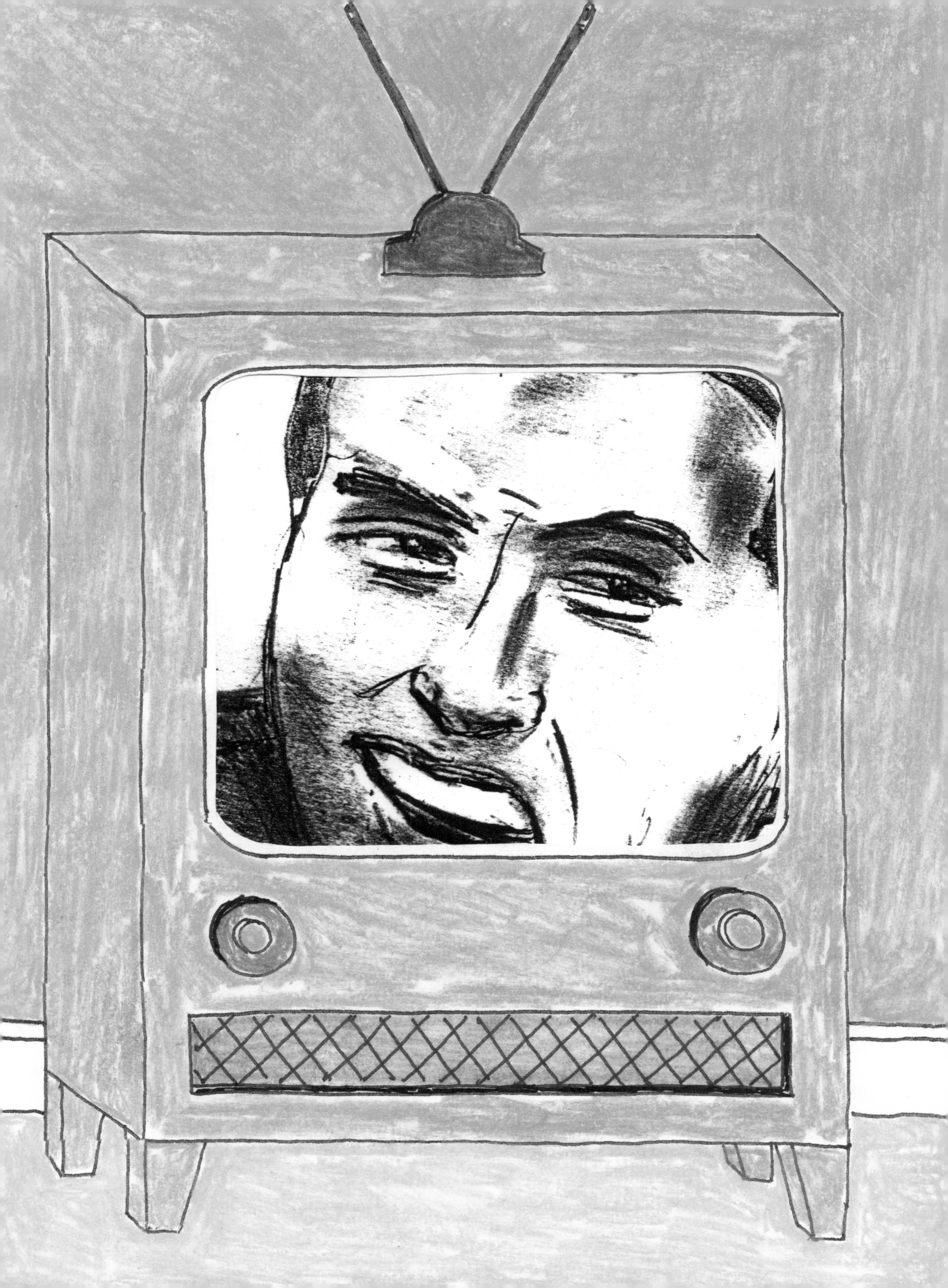

In the Army

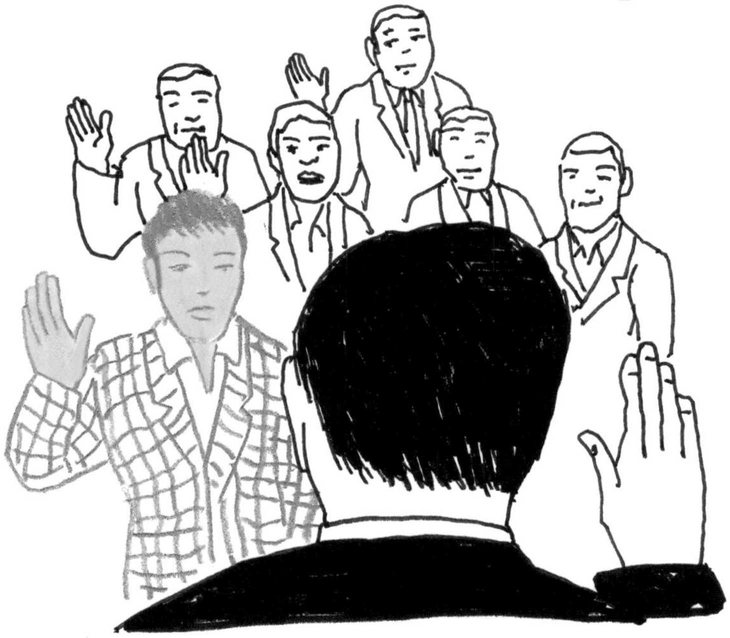

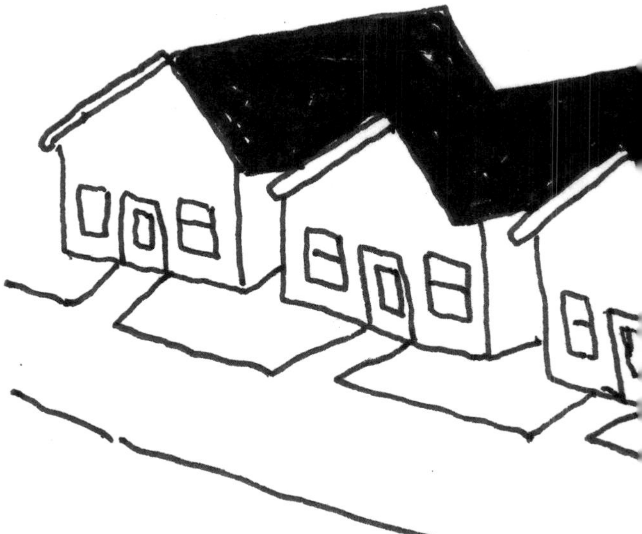

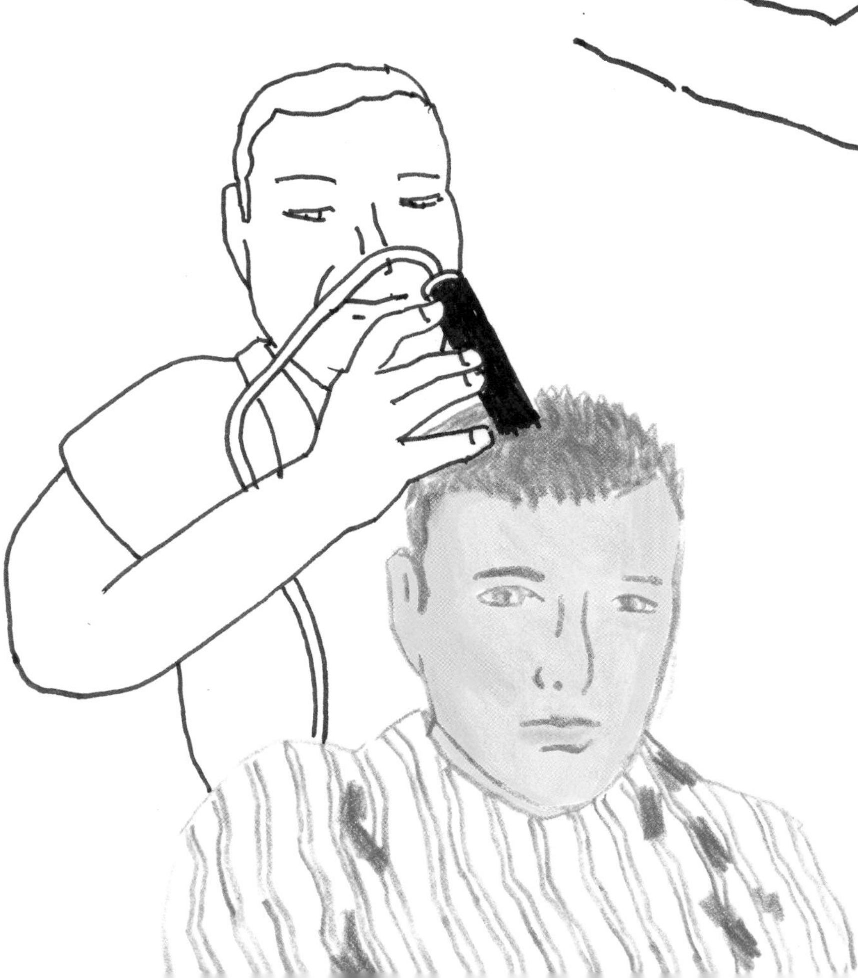

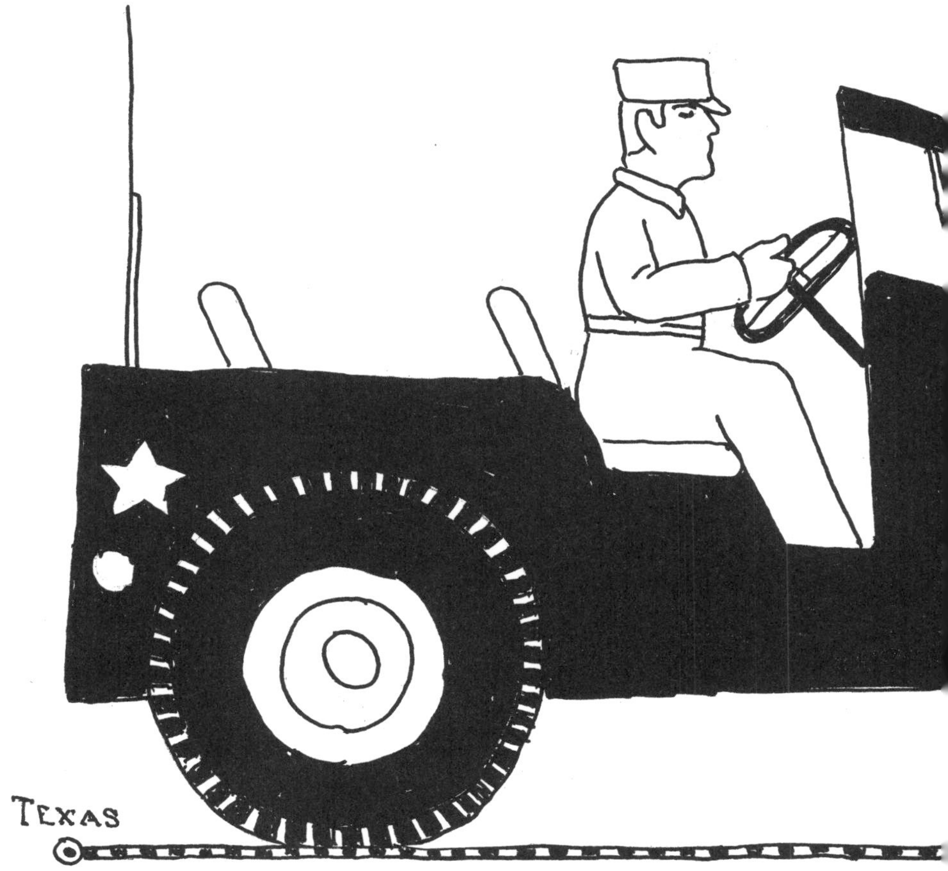
TEXAS

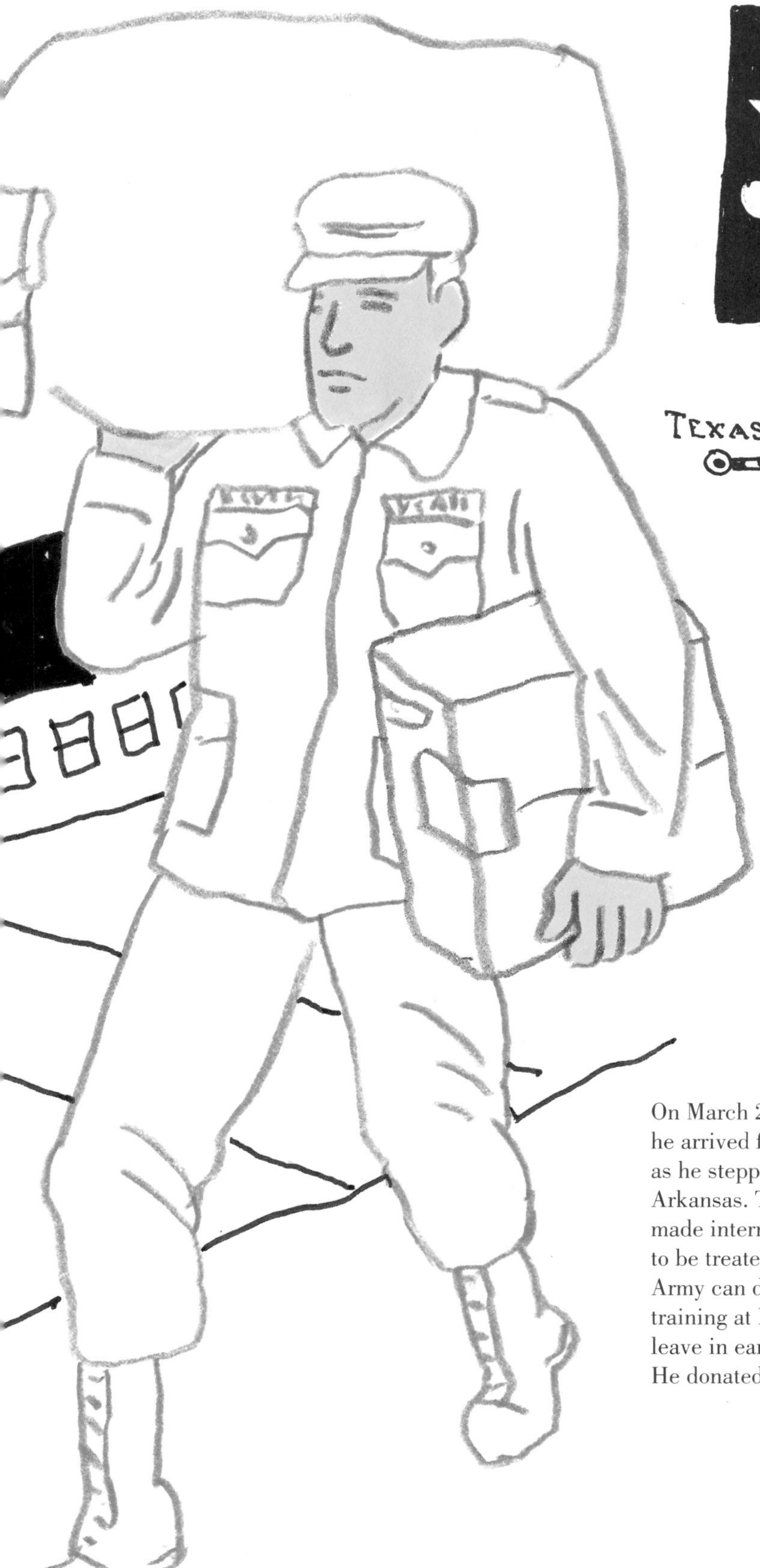

On March 24, 1958 Elvis is drafted into the army. When he arrived for induction, hundreds of people gathered as he stepped down from the bus at Fort Chaffee, Arkansas. There Elvis received a GI haircut, which made international news. Presley said he did not want to be treated any differently from anyone else, that "The Army can do anything it wants with me." He began basic training at Fort Hood, Texas, and during a two-week leave in early June he recorded five songs in Nashville. He donated his Army pay to charity.

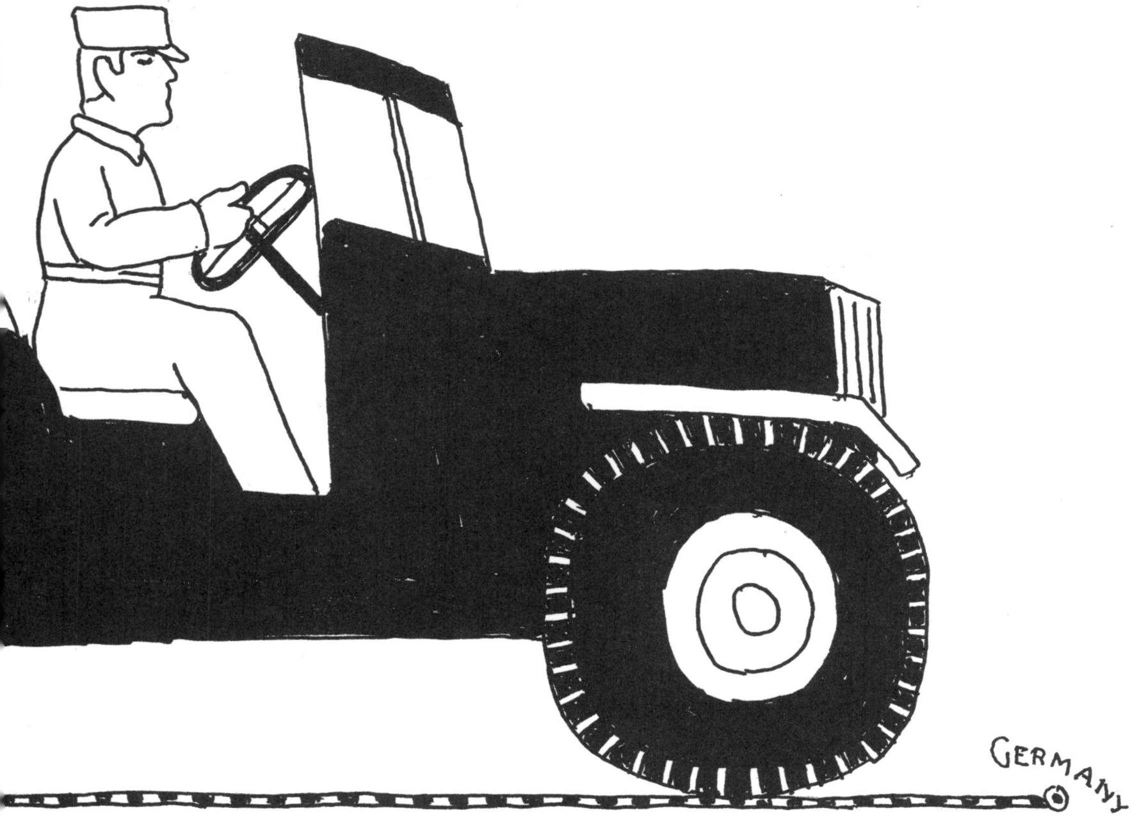
GERMANY

In August, Elvis' mother, Gladys, died from complications of hepatitis at age 46. Elvis was granted emergency leave to visit her and spent her last two days by her bedside. Elvis was crushed.

The next month Elvis shipped out on the USS *Randall* to serve 18 months of active duty in Germany. While on maneuvers, Presley was introduced to amphetamines by a sergeant. He also began to study karate. While stationed there Presley had ten top 40 hits with recordings he made prior to induction. On March 5, 1960 Elvis was discharged from active duty by the U.S. Army.

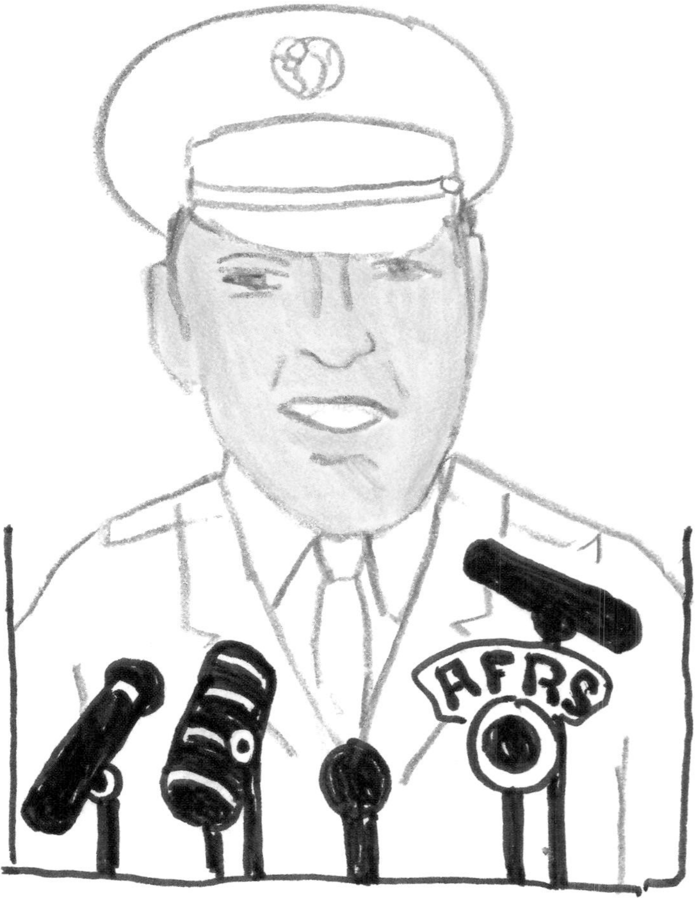
AFRS

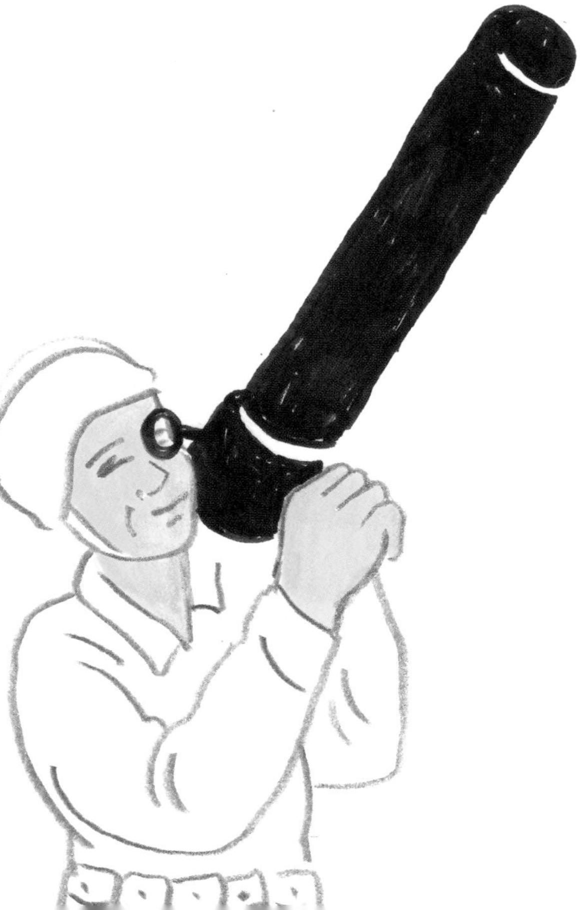

Graceland

The year before being drafted, Elvis purchased Graceland Mansion, located on a 13.8-acre estate in Memphis, Tennessee. Built in 1939, it was formerly owned by Stephen C. Toof, founder of S.C. Toof & Co., the oldest commercial printing firm in Memphis. As Presley's fame grew, a large number of fans and journalists would regularly congregate outside his house where he lived with his parents, to the annoyance of his neighbors. In 1957 he gave his parents a budget of $100,000 to find a new home. In March of that year Presley paid $102,500 for the mansion and grounds. They soon decorated the interior, replacing the pastel colored walls with the red and gold curtain décor it is known for. After the White House, Graceland is the second most-visited house in America, with over 650,000 visitors per year.

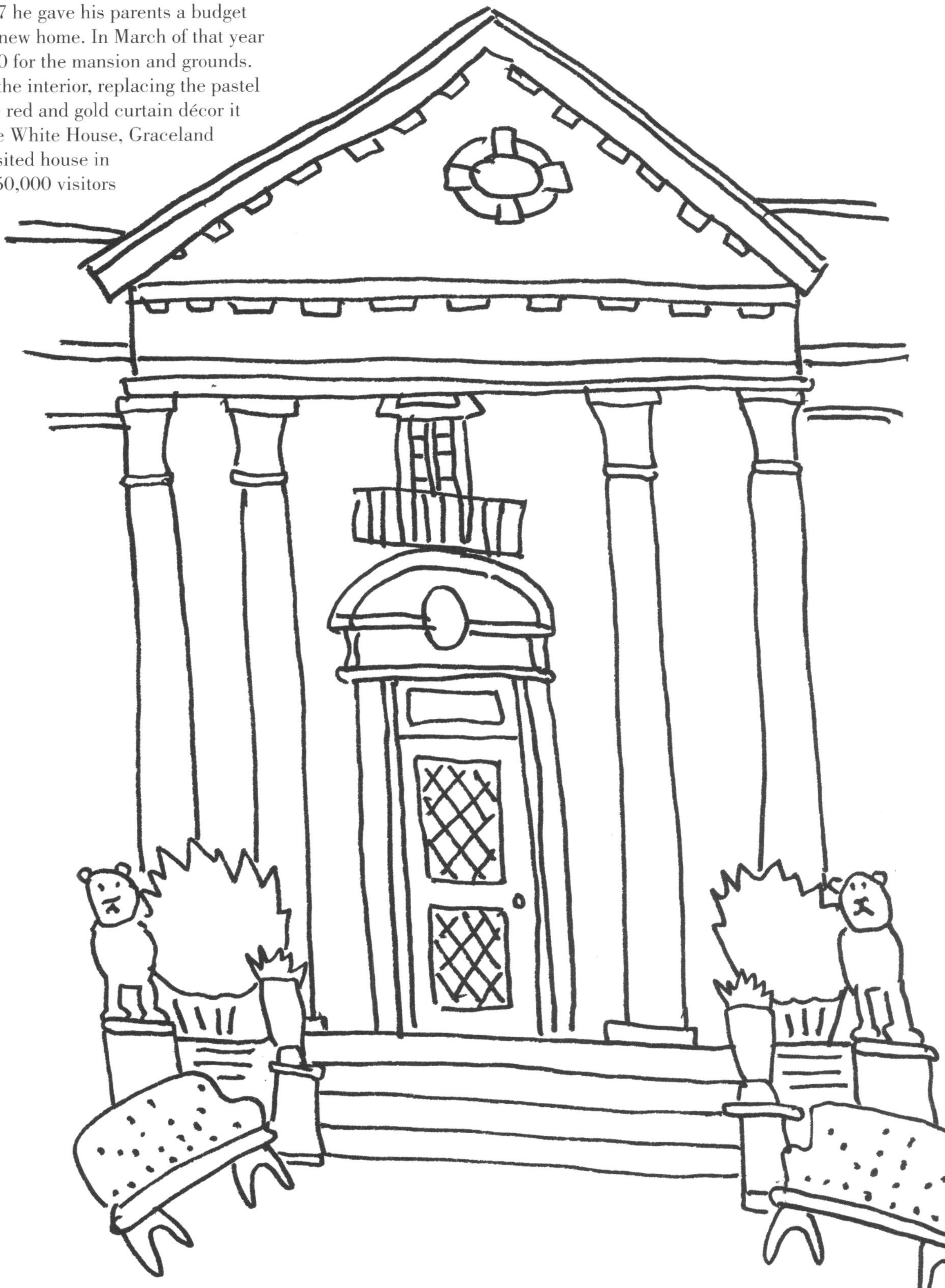

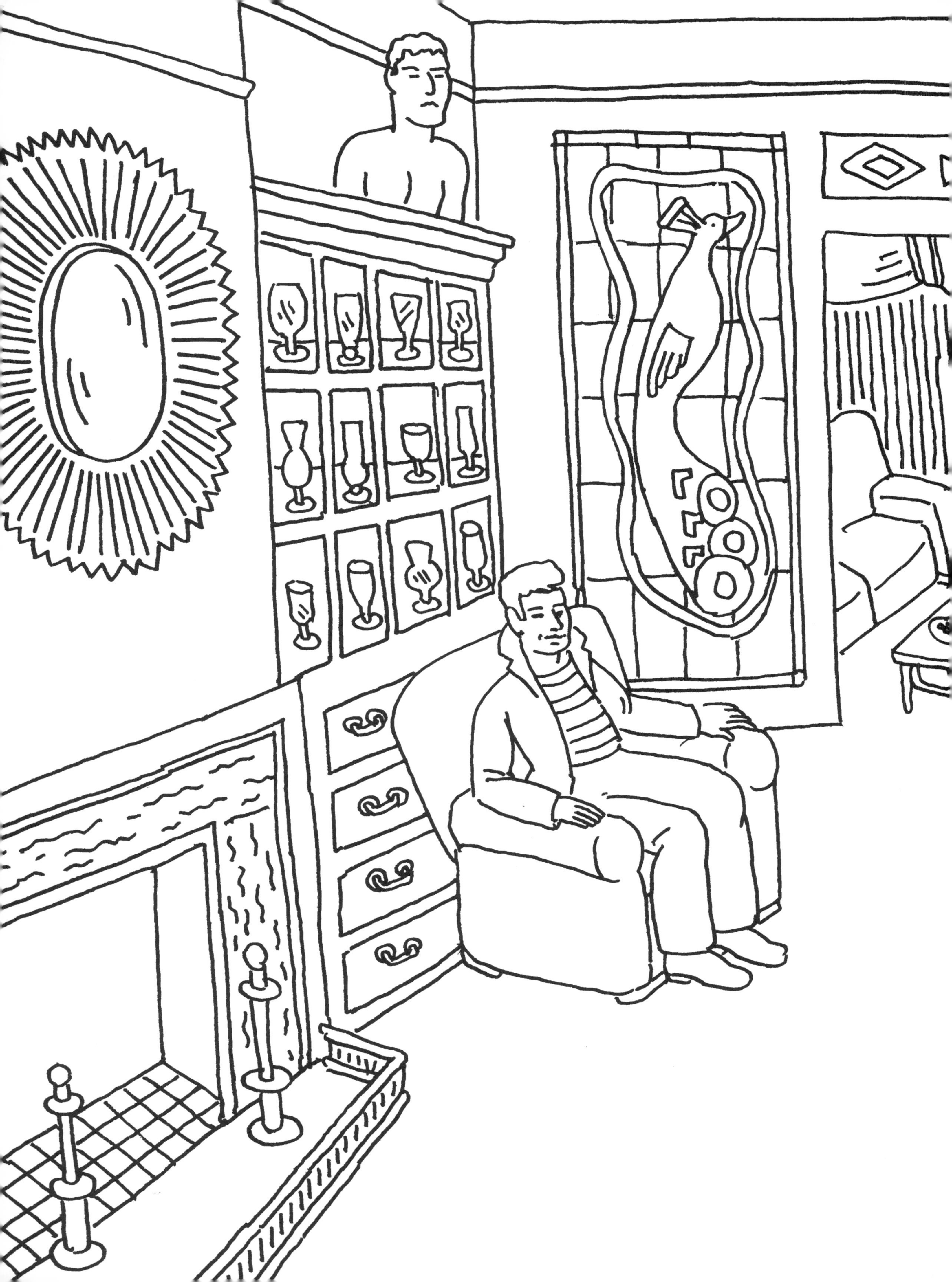

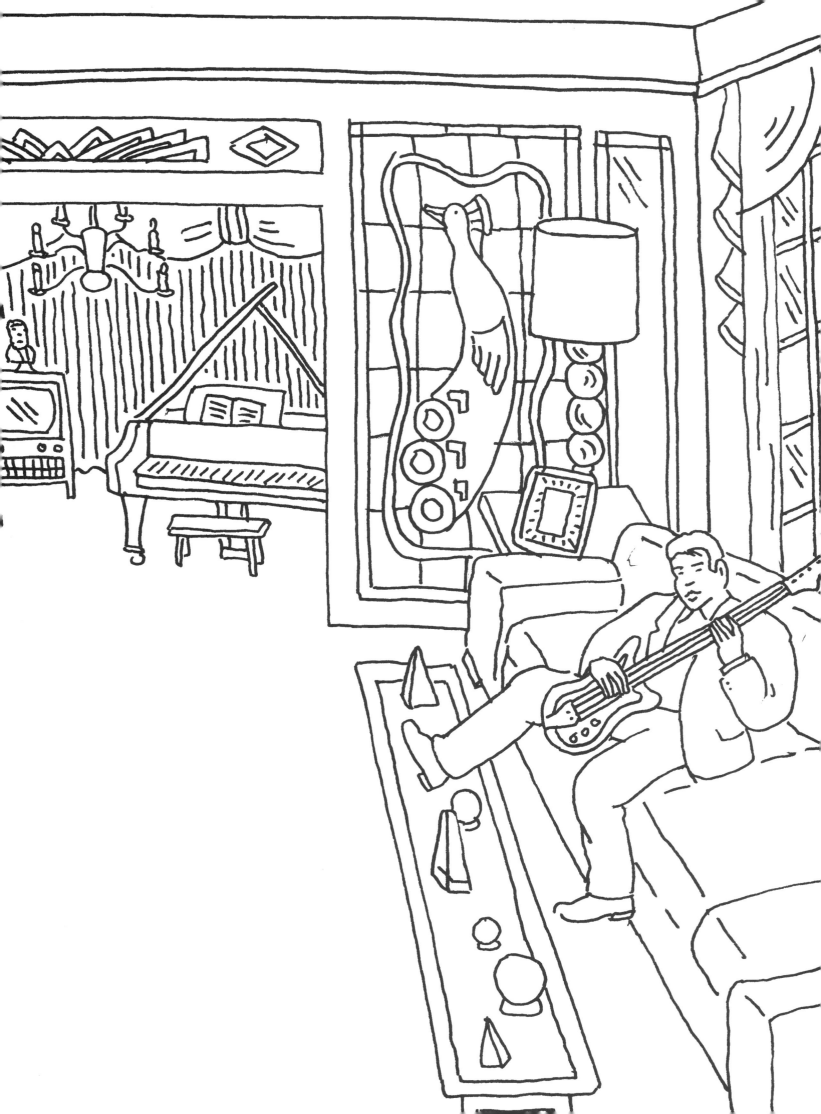

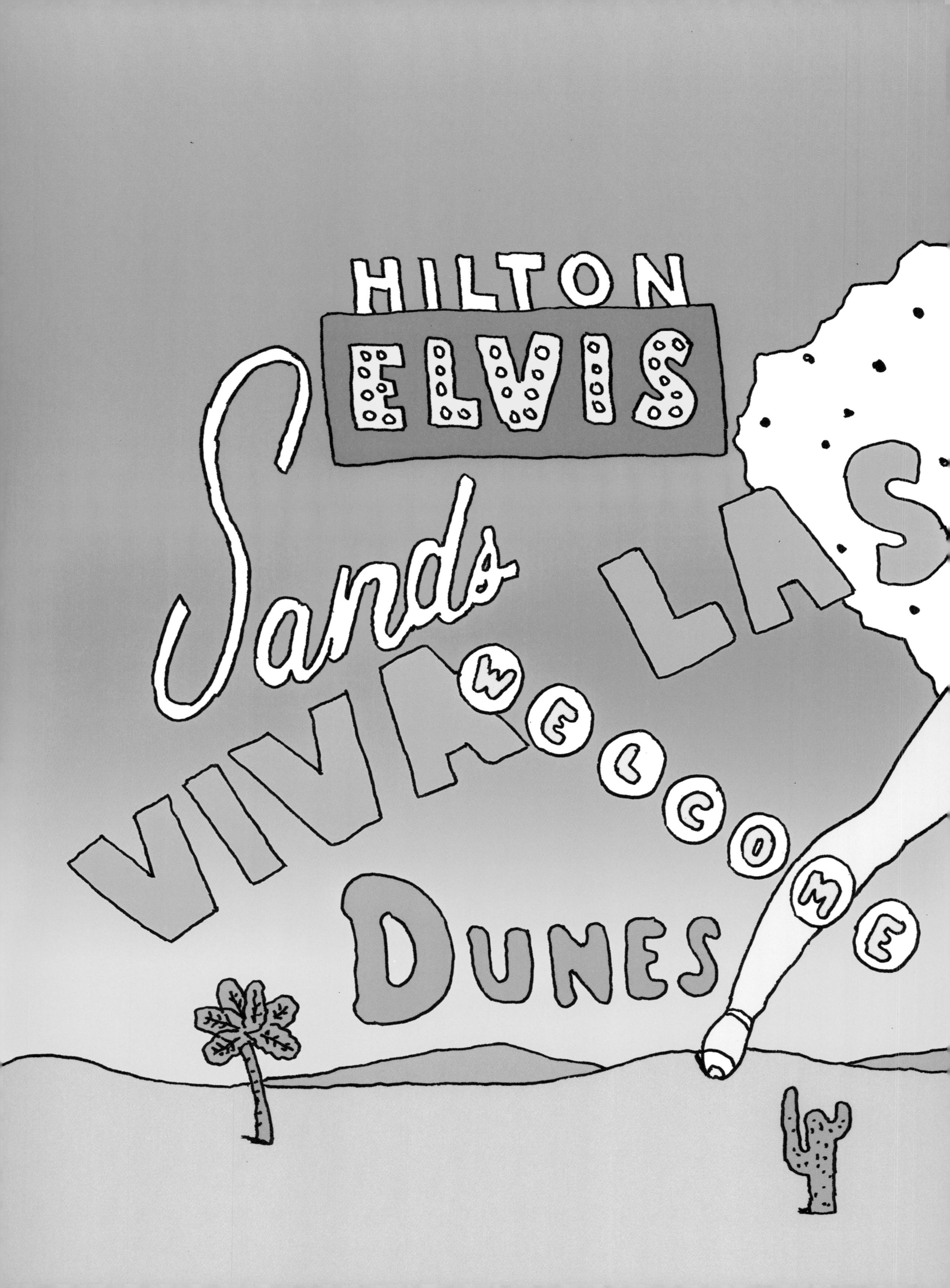
HILTON
ELVIS
Sands
VIVA LAS
WELCOME
DUNES

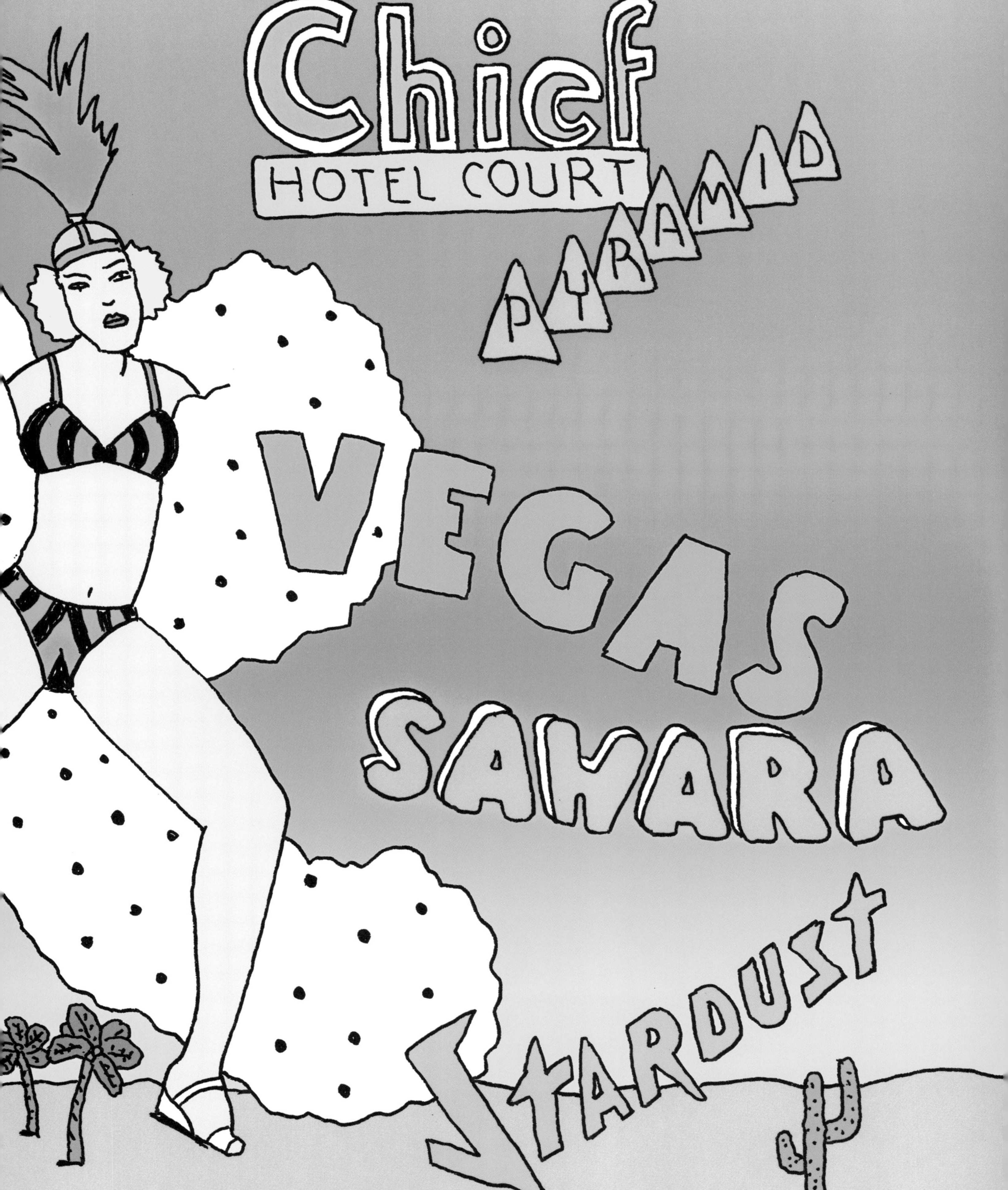
Chief
HOTEL COURT
PYRAMID
VEGAS
SAHARA
STARDUST

Frank Sinatra

Like many of the older generation, Frank Sinatra was at first threatened by Elvis, declaring his music "deplorable," but was soon singing a different tune.

Elvis' first television appearance following his army stint, was on May 12th, 1960, on *The Frank Sinatra Timex Show*, with the special entitled "Welcome Home, Elvis." Colonel Parker demanded $125,000 for two songs, a total of eight minutes on screen. Sinatra himself received a lower sum for the whole show. The show began with Presley in his Army uniform but the highlight of the show was a duet between the two musical stars, with Sinatra singing lines from "Love Me Tender" and Presley lyrics from "Witchcraft." The show also starred Rat Packers Sammy Davis Jr. and Joey Bishop and Frank's daughter Nancy, who would later co-star with Elvis in "Speedway." It earned an impressive 41.5% of the evenings' ratings.

The two never worked together again, but kept in touch over the years. Sinatra let Elvis and Priscilla borrow his private jet in 1967 to fly from Palm Springs to Las Vegas for their wedding, and to travel back to Palm Springs for their honeymoon. A staple of later Presley performances was his cover of Sinatra's song, "My Way."

In 1977, following Elvis' passing, Sinatra would go on record to state, "There have been many accolades uttered about Elvis' talent and performances through the years, all of which I agree with wholeheartedly. I shall miss him dearly as a friend. He was a warm, considerate and generous man."

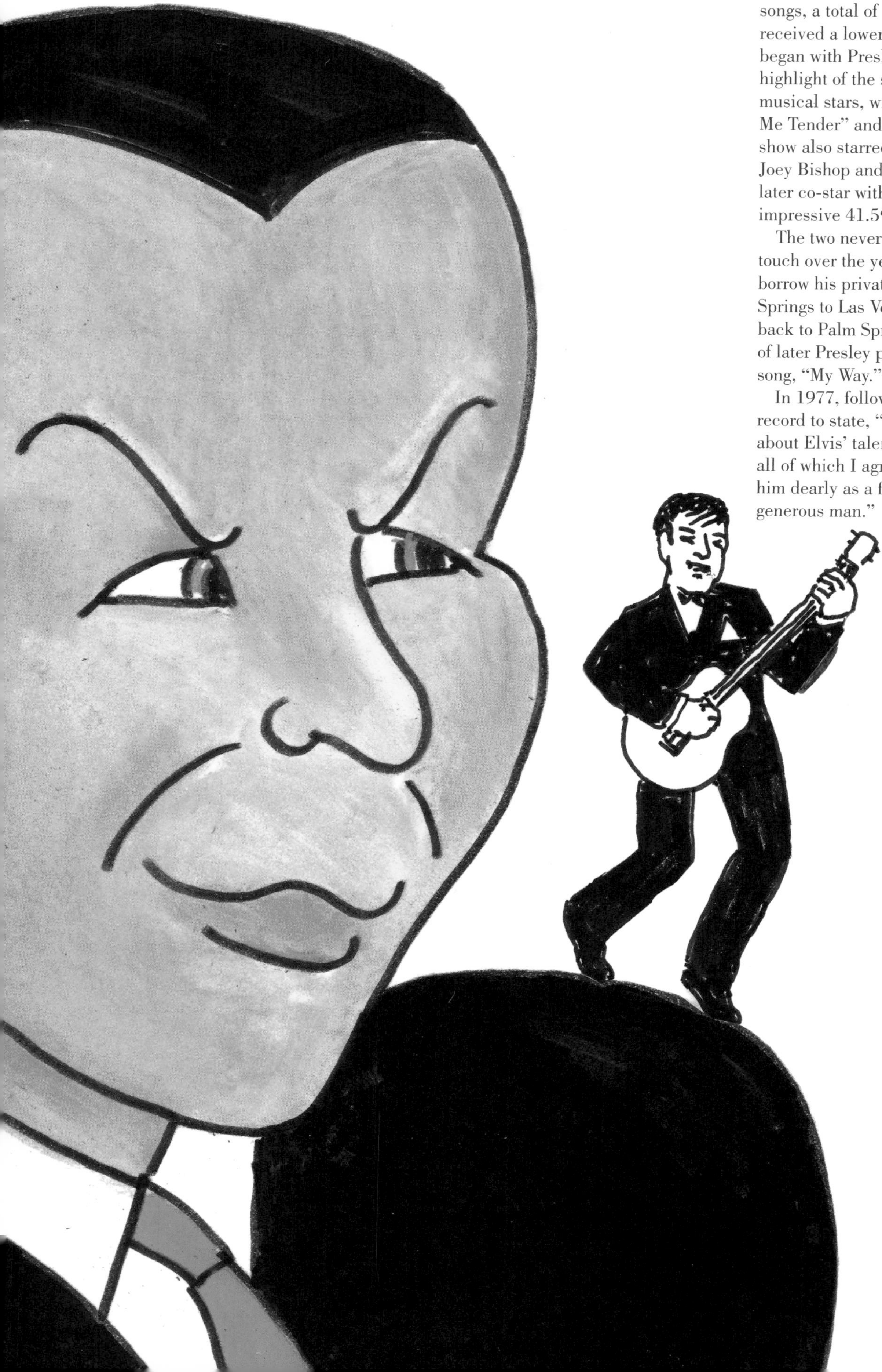

Concerts

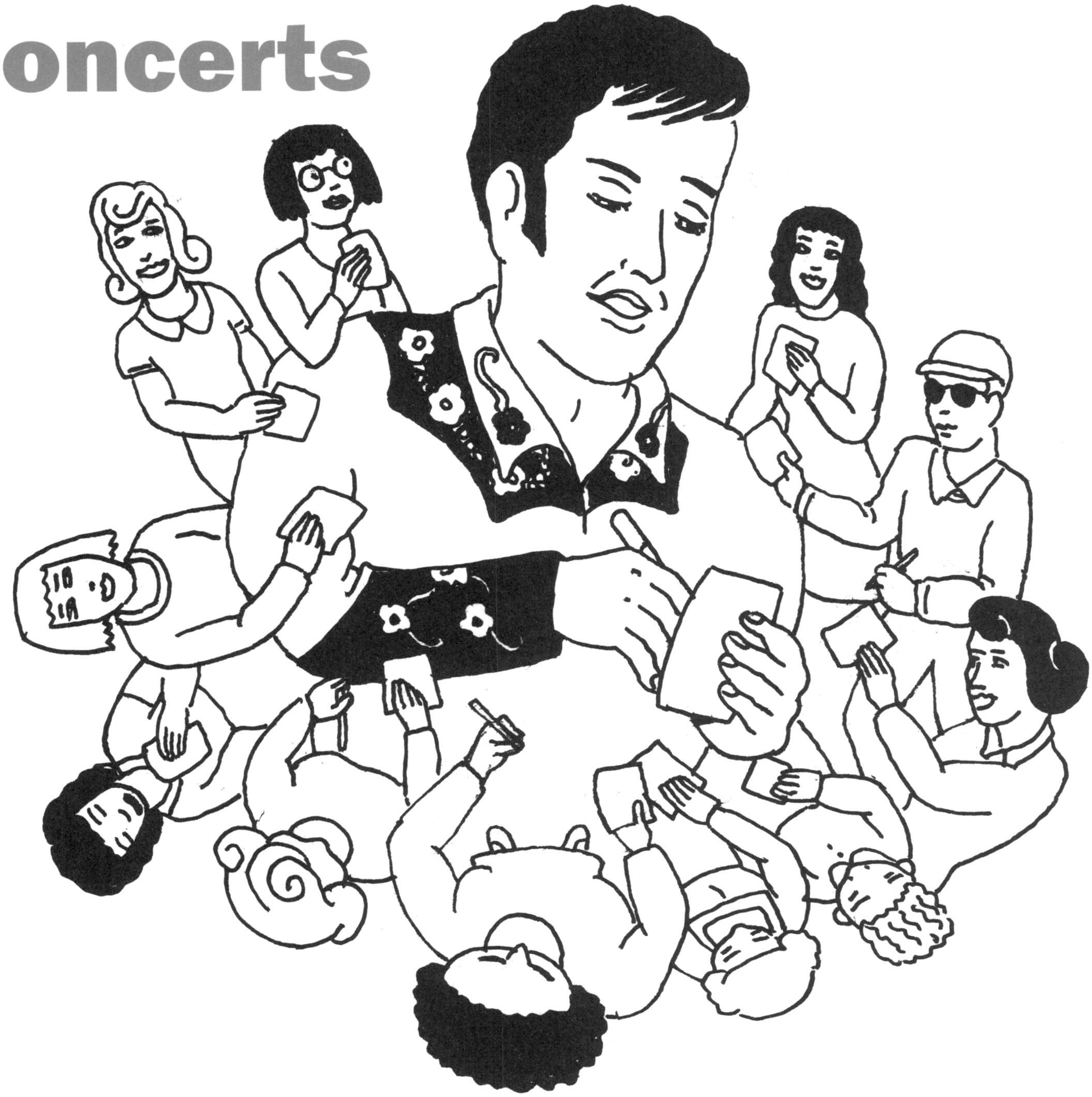

Elvis' first live appearances featured the stripped-down trio, guitarist Scotty Moore, bass player Bill Black and Elvis. In July 1954, Elvis, Scotty and Bill performed to the Bon Air Club, and later that month at Overton Park Shell in Memphis and the crowd went wild. This was followed in October with an appearance on Nashville's *Grand Ole Opry*, which was greeted by only a polite audience response. Two weeks later, Presley and company appeared on the *Louisiana Hayride*, the *Opry*'s rival. They are joined on stage by steel guitar player Sonny Trammel and, for the second set, house drummer D. J. Fontana, who would remain as Presley's drummer. The audience jumped to their feet and shrieked. The show was broadcast to 198 radio stations in 28 states. Following that appearance, the *Hayride* engaged Presley for a year's worth of Saturday-night appearances.

In 1955 Elvis joined Hank Snow's national tour. In Odessa, Texas, a 19-year-old Roy Orbison was in the audience. "His energy was incredible; his instinct was just amazing...I just didn't know what to make of it. There was just no reference point in the culture to compare it." However, the reaction of teenage boys jealous of their girlfriend's reactions to Elvis' animated performances and gyrations caused the band to enlist the help of police guards. In September of 1956 fifty National Guardsmen were added to the police security to protect the star.

On March 25, 1961, Elvis performed at a benefit concert at the Bloch Arena in Pearl Harbor, Hawaii to raise money for the Memorial to the USS *Arizona*, which was sunk in the attack on Pearl Harbor. This was Presley's last public performance for seven years.

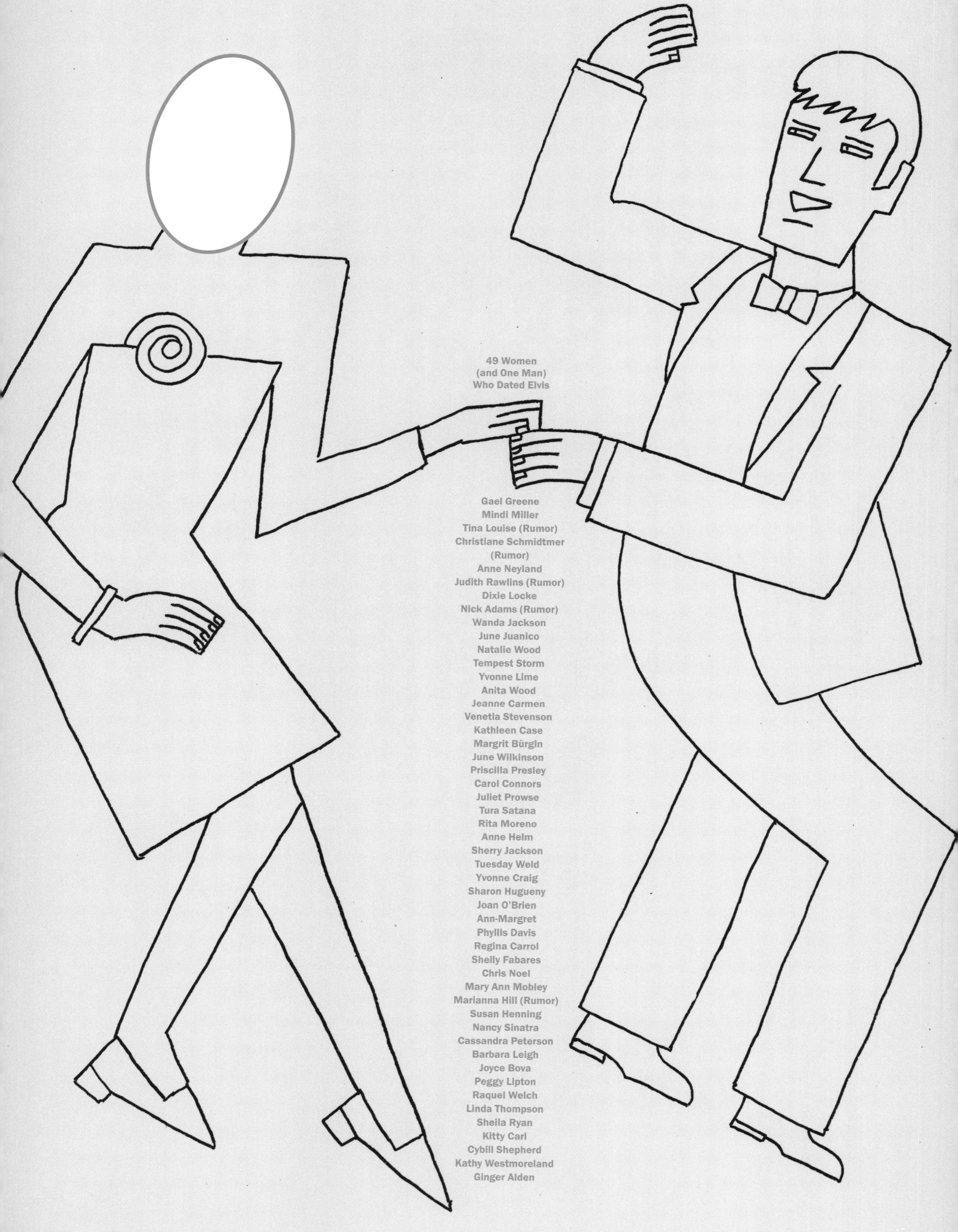

49 Women
(and One Man)
Who Dated Elvis

Gael Greene
Mindi Miller
Tina Louise (Rumor)
Christiane Schmidtmer
(Rumor)
Anne Neyland
Judith Rawlins (Rumor)
Dixie Locke
Nick Adams (Rumor)
Wanda Jackson
June Juanico
Natalie Wood
Tempest Storm
Yvonne Lime
Anita Wood
Jeanne Carmen
Venetia Stevenson
Kathleen Case
Margrit Bürgin
June Wilkinson
Priscilla Presley
Carol Connors
Juliet Prowse
Tura Satana
Rita Moreno
Anne Helm
Sherry Jackson
Tuesday Weld
Yvonne Craig
Sharon Hugueny
Joan O'Brien
Ann-Margret
Phyllis Davis
Regina Carrol
Shelly Fabares
Chris Noel
Mary Ann Mobley
Marianna Hill (Rumor)
Susan Henning
Nancy Sinatra
Cassandra Peterson
Barbara Leigh
Joyce Bova
Peggy Lipton
Raquel Welch
Linda Thompson
Sheila Ryan
Kitty Carl
Cybill Shepherd
Kathy Westmoreland
Ginger Alden

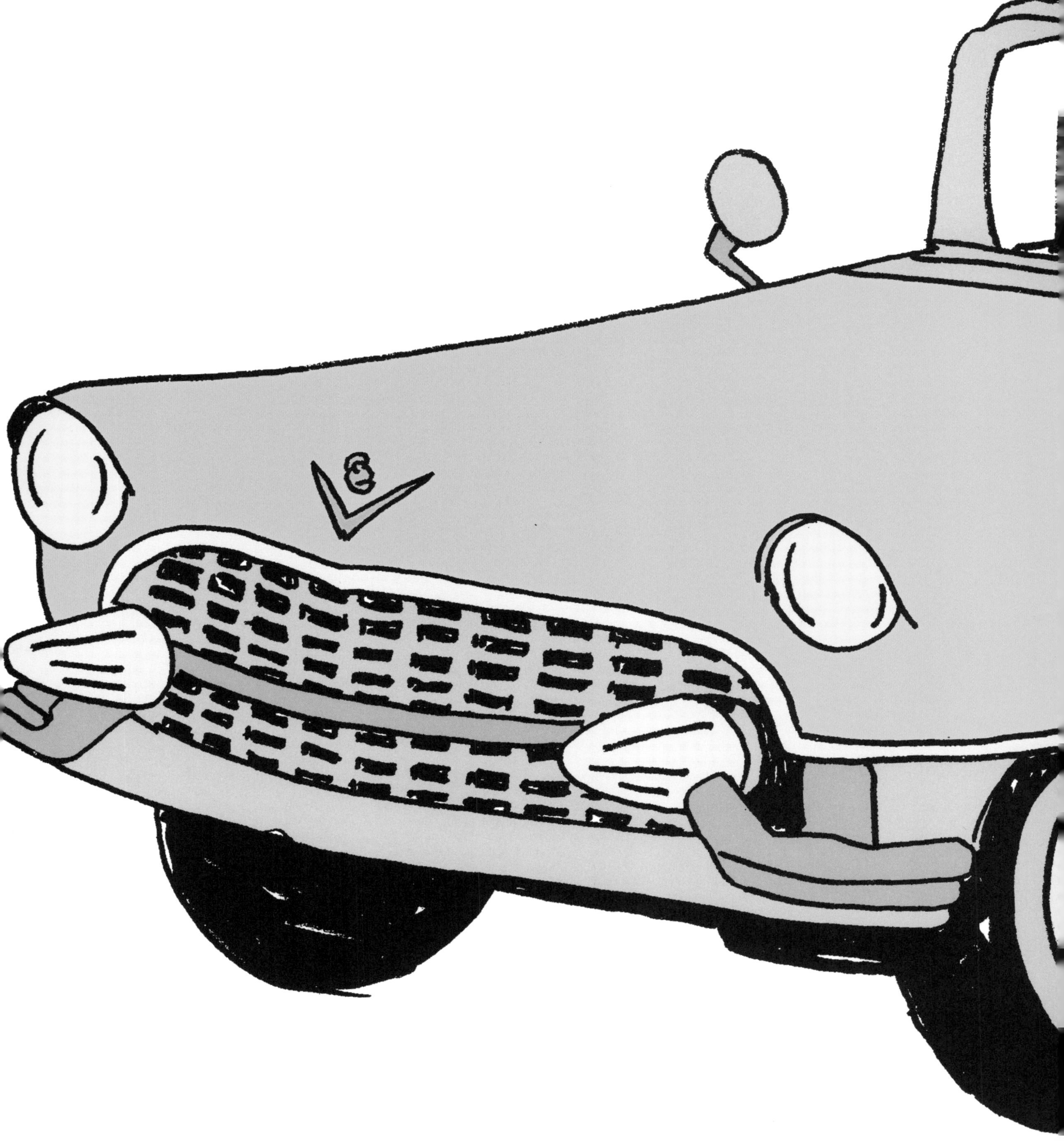

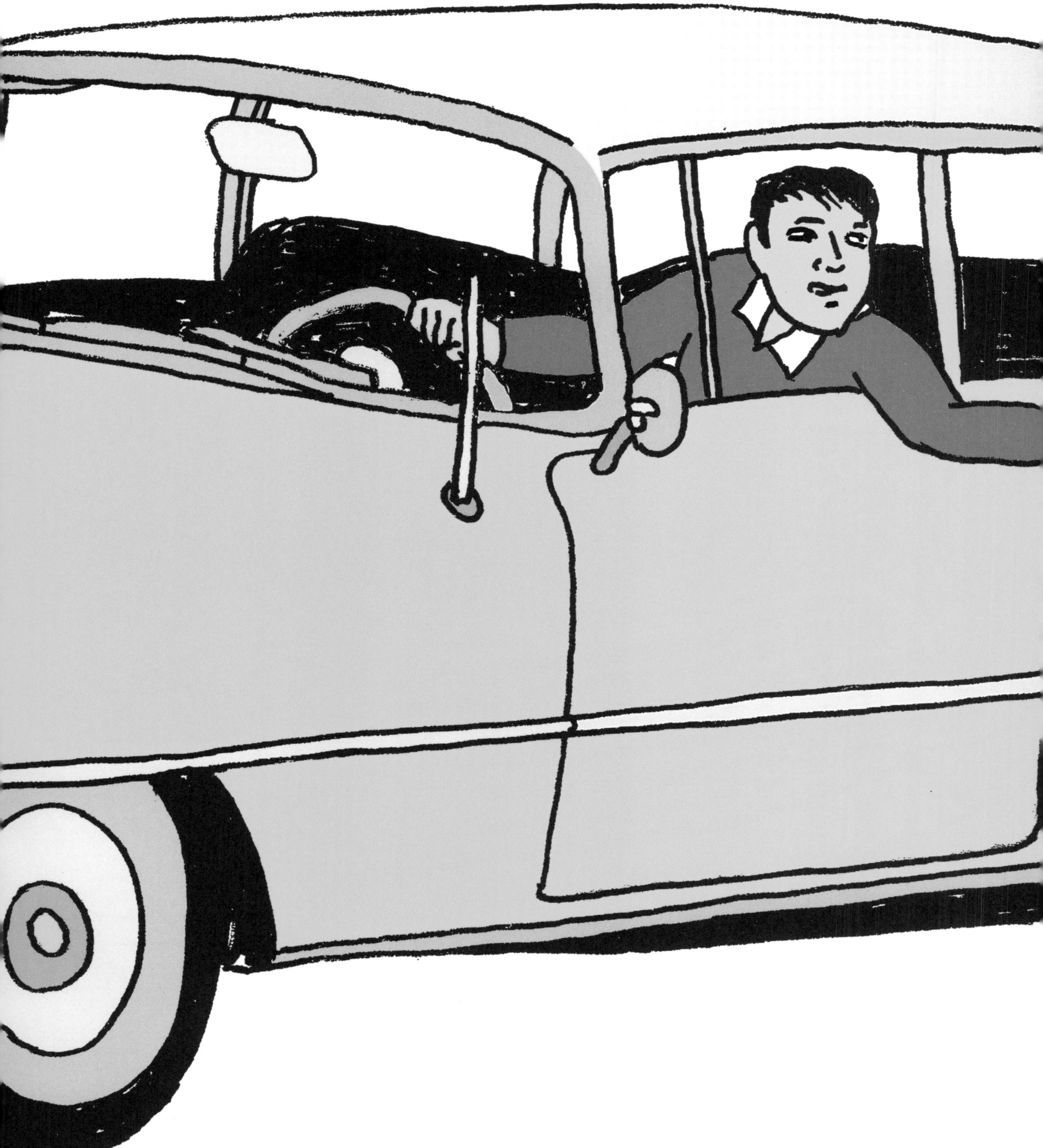

Pink Cadillac

One of the first things Elvis did after his initial success was to purchase a 1954 Fleetwood Series 60 pink Cadillac in early 1955. The car caught fire later that year due to a faulty brake line. He replaced it with another Cadillac of the same series, but blue with a black roof. He had the new car repainted pink and presented it to his mother as a gift, the first of many such gifts to friends, body guards, karate instructors, his hair stylist, family and others over the years. The exact number is unknown, but it is believed he gave away as many as 200. One of the original pink Cadillacs remains on permanent display at Graceland.

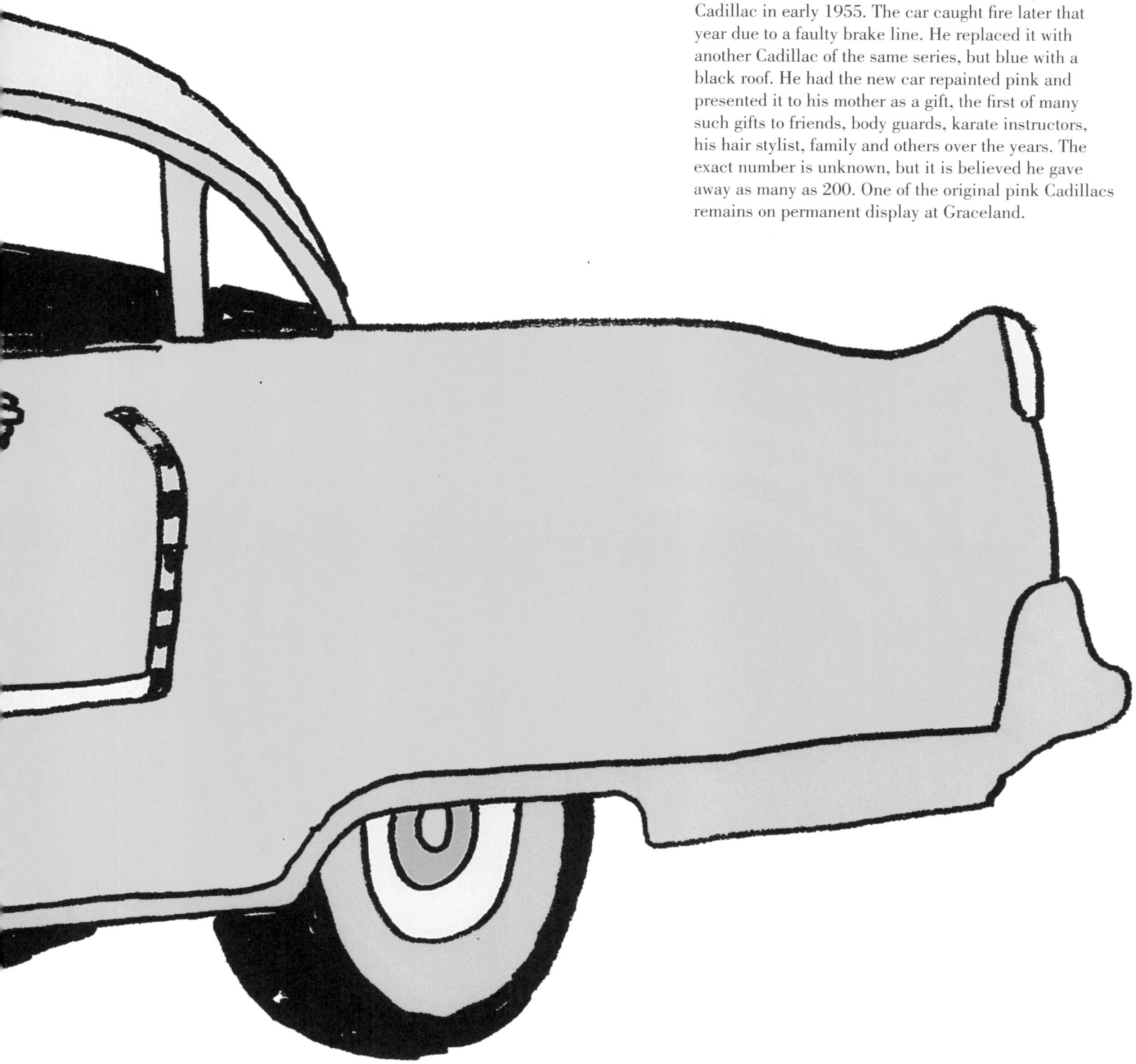

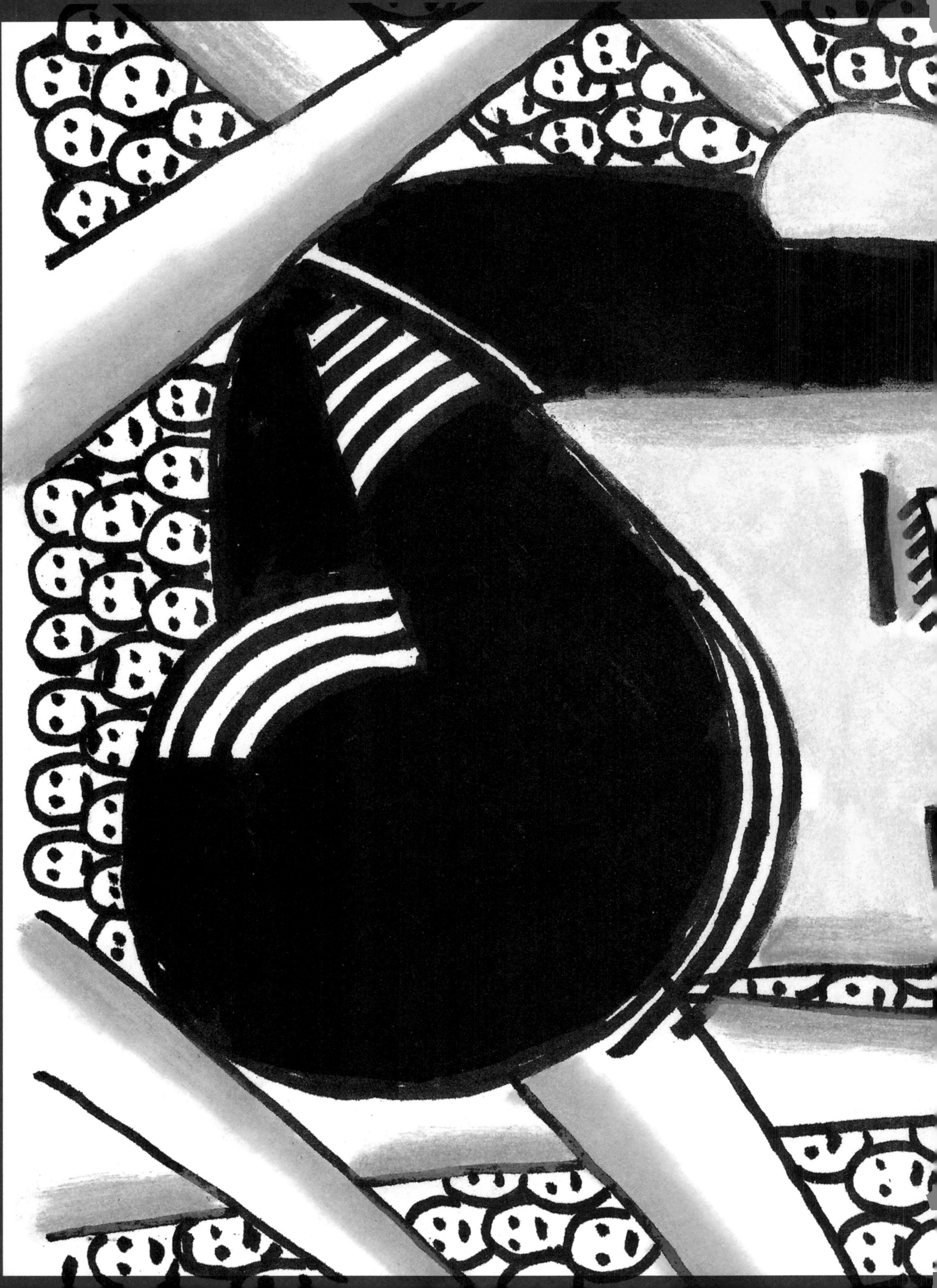

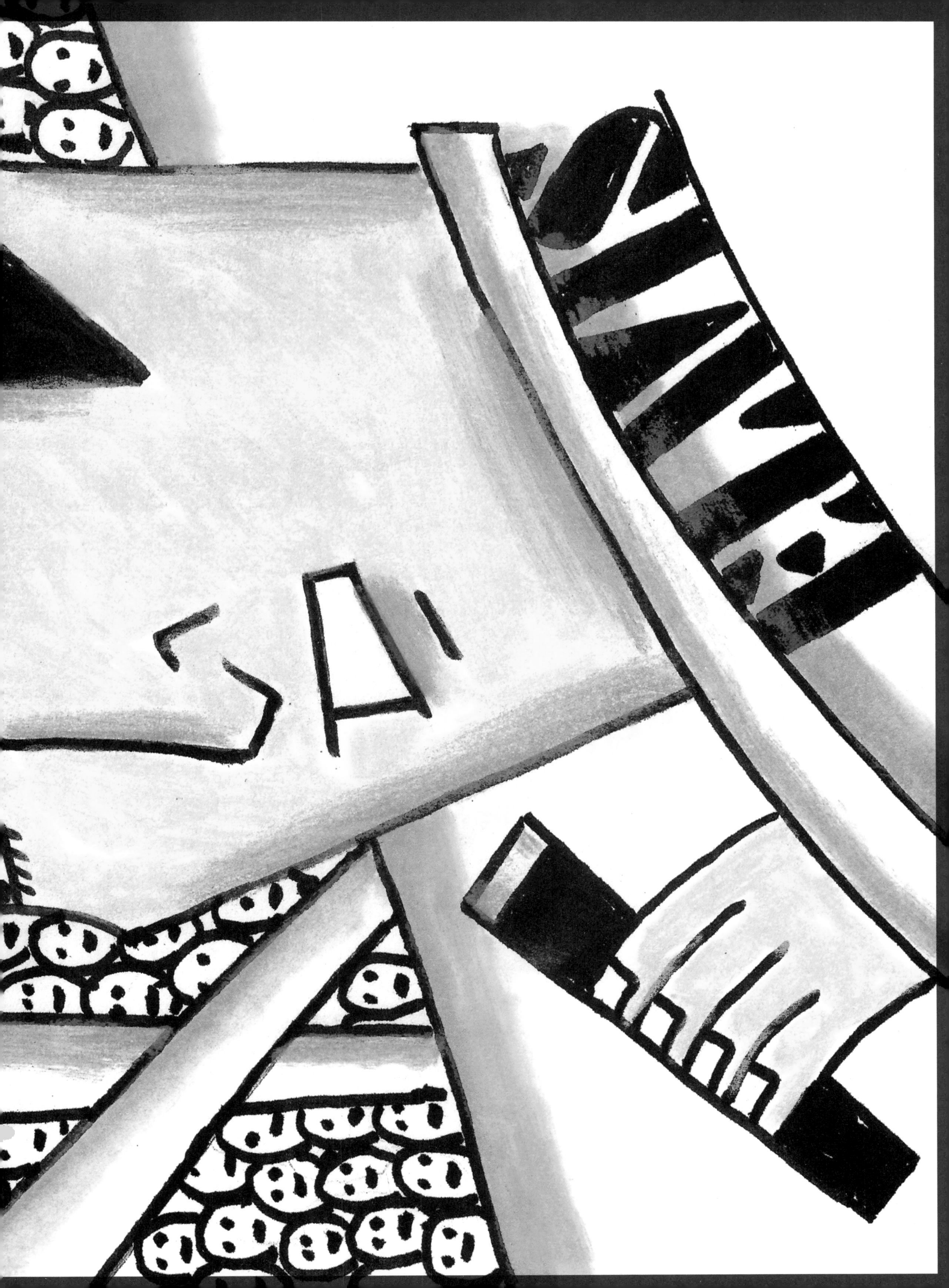

Masculine Idols/Heroes

The post-war rebellion was personified by Marlon Brando in 1953 in the original outlaw biker film *The Wild One*. In character, in response to "Hey Johnny, what are you rebelling against?," he sullenly replied, "Whaddaya got?"

Likewise, James Dean typified teenage angst in the first two of his three films, *East of Eden* and *Rebel Without a Cause*, both released in 1955 with gut-wrenching emotional performances. In the latter he wore his now famous red jacket with the collar turned up, foreshadowing Elvis' high-collared jumpsuits by two decades.

When asked if he will be the next James Dean, in his now infamous 1956 television interview on *Hy Gardner Calling*, a heavy lidded Elvis replied, "I would never compare myself in any way to James Dean because James Dean was a genius at acting."

Elvis would meet his other idol, Brando, at the Paramount commissary during the filming of "King Creole." Brando came in and sat behind Presley. Co-star Jan Shepard told Elvis who was sitting behind him and Elvis looked as if he wanted to hide under the table. According to Shepard they shook hands, wished each other luck with their respective films, and Elvis "was very cool…we get outside and he jumped at least five feet in the air. He could not believe he shook hands with Marlon Brando." After its opening, a review of *King Creole* ran with the headline, "A Bourbon Street Brando." Shepard recalled that Elvis "was very proud of that, very happy."

A less likely, yet key influence on Presley was Dean Martin. With his swarthy good looks, jet black pomaded hair combed into a pompadour, and smooth personality, Elvis would tell Dean's daughter, "They call me the King of Rock and Roll, but your dad is the King of Cool."

James Dean

Dean Martin

Marlon Brando

Elvis Presley

39

Films

Elvis desired to become a serious actor, like his film idols Marlon Brando and James Dean. Sadly, this was not to be. He was off to a good start in 1956 with the black and white Western *Love Me Tender*, starring Richard Egan and Debra Paget. Presley received third billing but the promotions for the film featured him heavily. Originally titled *The Reno Brothers*, the name was changed after Presley's hit sold over a million copies. At the insistence of Colonel Parker, four songs were included that were stylistically incongruent for the post Civil War era portrayed.

He followed this up the next year as the headliner in the Technicolor *Loving You*, co-starring former film siren Lizabeth Scott. This time out Elvis stayed closer to

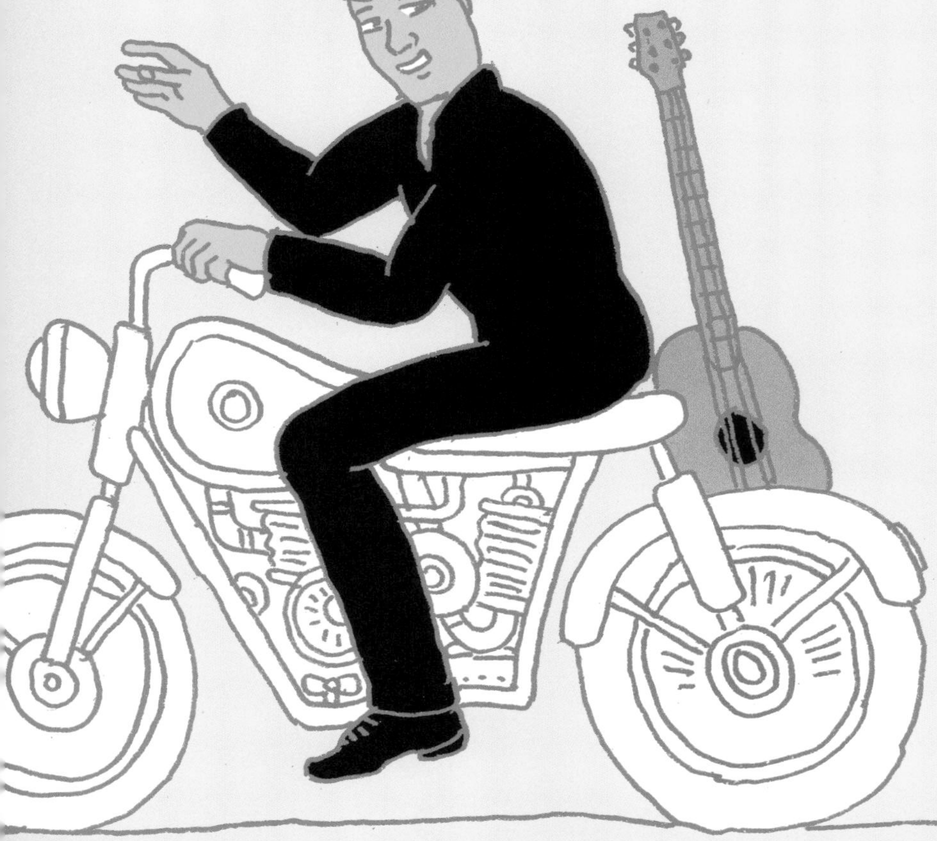

Roustabout
1963

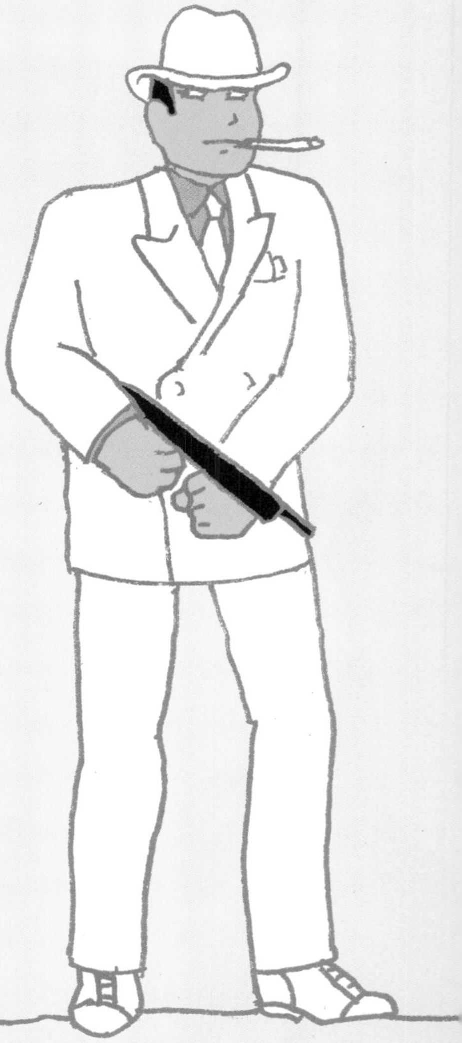

The Trouble with Girls
1969

home, portraying a singer and delivery man who achieves musical stardom.

In November 1958 *Jailhouse Rock*, Elvis' third motion picture, opened nationally. Presley choreographed the famous prison dance scene, which has become indelibly etched into the popular culture consciousness.

It is his fourth film, however, that many consider his best. *King Creole*, directed by Oscar-winning Hollywood veteran Michael Curtiz (*Casablanca*). It costarred Carolyn Jones, Walter Matthau, and Dean Jagger. Based on Harold Robbins' 1952 novel, *A Stone for Danny Fisher*, Elvis played the title role of Danny. According to a review in *Billboard*, "Elvis Presley's new film shapes up as a box-office winner. It's got plenty of action…and the star gives his best acting performance to date."

Regrettably, following this success, the films became increasingly formulaic (boy meets girl, boy sings, boy overcomes difficulty, boy gets girl), perhaps due to the fact that he cranked out 27 of them over the next nine years. Possibly it was in reaction to his more dramatic films being less commercially successful than his lighter fair, or the success of his musical comedy soundtracks, but Presley increasingly appeared to be performing by rote, both in his acting and recordings. Still, in June 1964, *Viva Las Vegas* outranked The Beatles' *A Hard Day's Night* at the box office and became Elvis' highest grossing film ever.

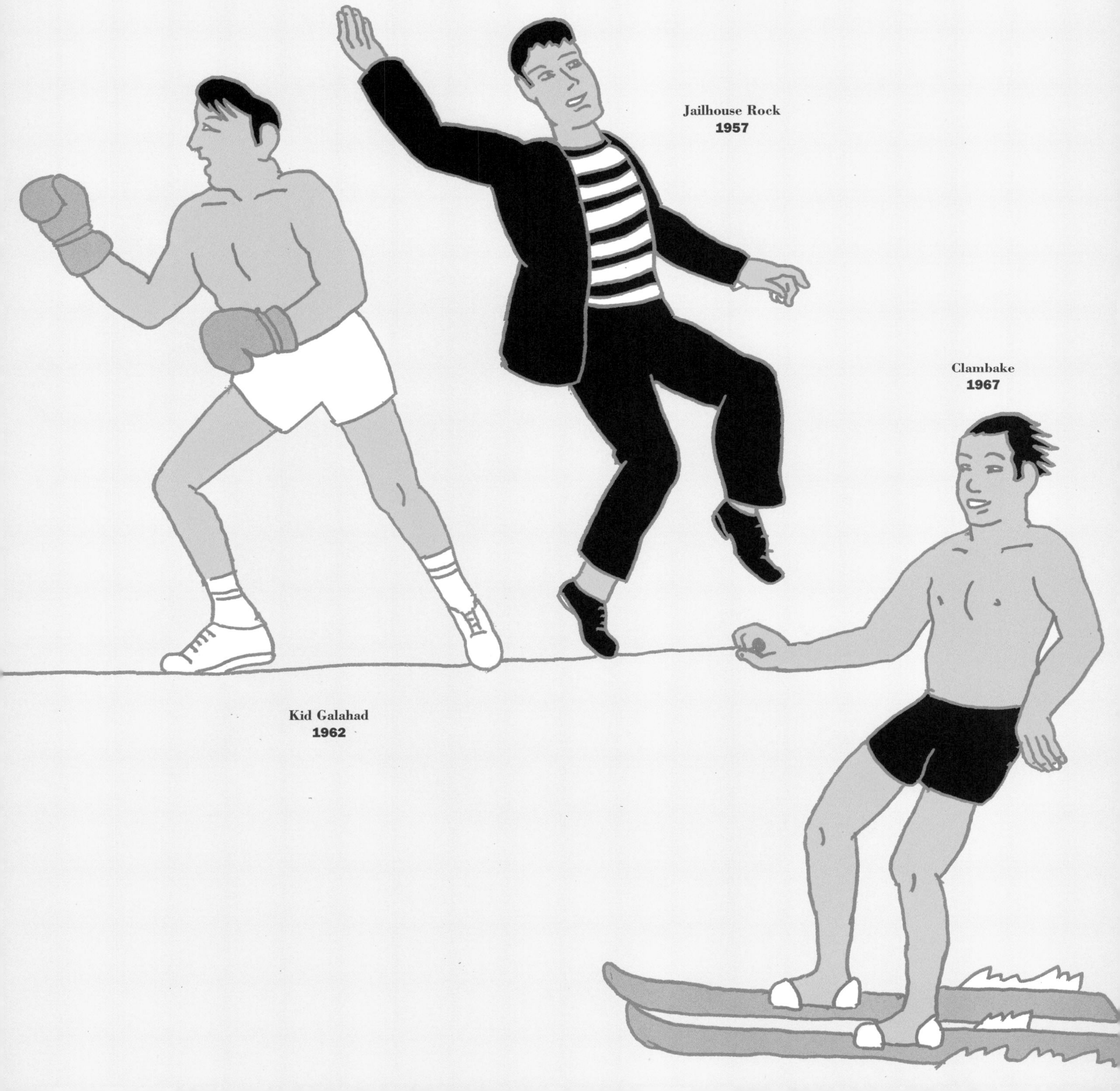
Jailhouse Rock
1957
Clambake
1967
Kid Galahad
1962

Comeback

On December 3, 1968 his eponymously named comeback television special *Elvis* aired on NBC to great ratings. Elvis was back! The following January Elvis returned to the recording studio in Memphis. The session produced four hit singles, "In The Ghetto," "Don't Cry Daddy," "Suspicious Minds," and "Kentucky Rain." In early 1970 he performed at the Annual Texas Livestock Show at the Houston Astrodome, breaking previous attendance records. He began touring for the first time since the 1950s. In June 1972 Elvis performed four sold out shows at New York's Madison Square Garden, setting ticket sales records. John Lennon, George Harrison, Bob Dylan, David Bowie, and Art Garfunkel were in the audience.

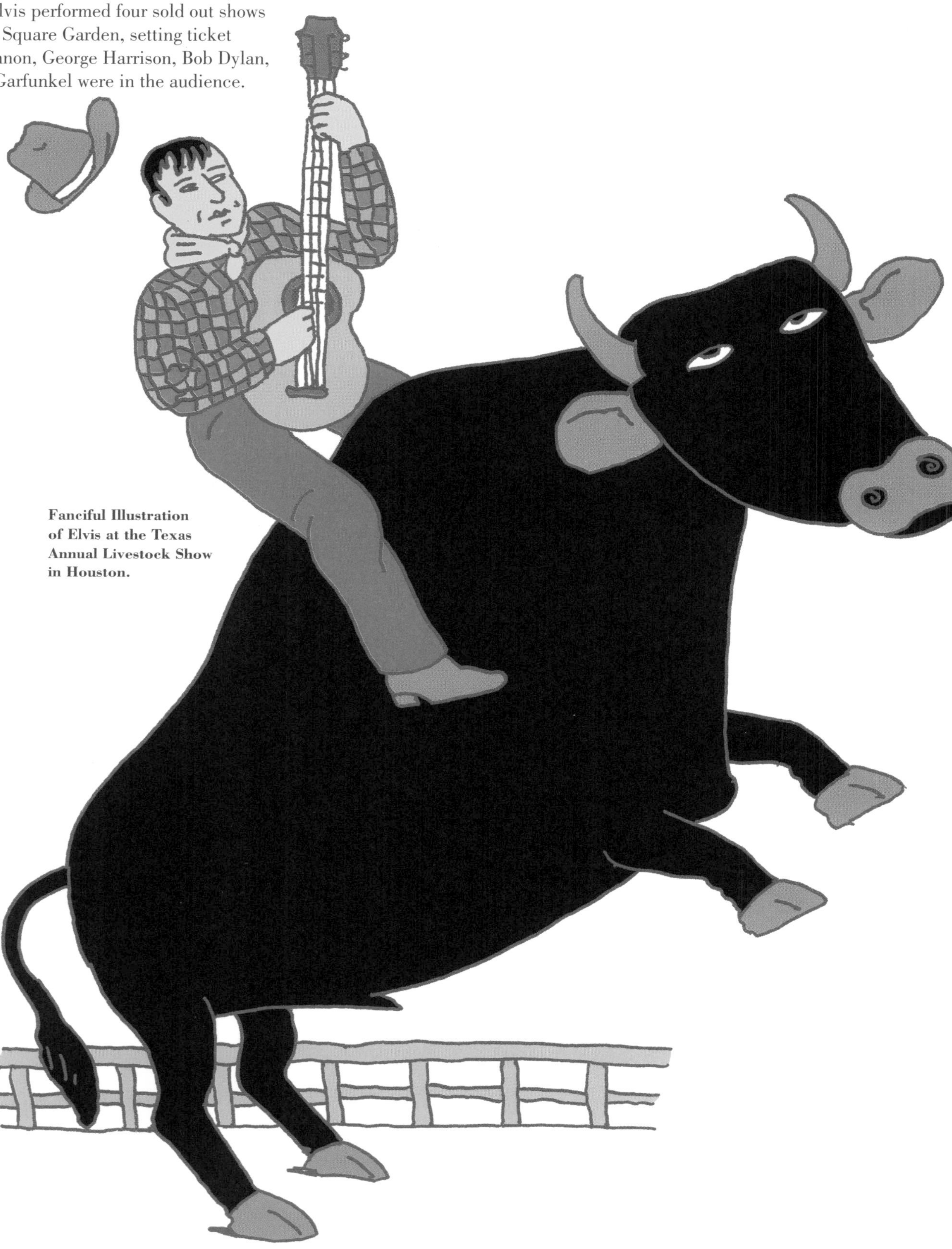

Fanciful Illustration of Elvis at the Texas Annual Livestock Show in Houston.

The Beatles

On March 22, 1963, The Beatles first album was released and topped the charts; the British Invasion had begun in the United Kingdom. While they did covers of Chuck Berry, Sun recording artist Carl Perkins, made the most of Buddy-Holly-like melodies and named themselves after his Crickets, the influence of Elvis was harder to discern. Yet, at a press conference in 1964, when asked about the comment that people think "you are nothing but a bunch of British Elvis Presleys," Ringo and John comically aped his classic gyrations to the delight of the crowd.

One has to dig deeper, to the days before their initial wholesome image was crystallized, to the sullen black and white photos of the "Silver Beatles" in Hamburg, with their high pompadours, black leather jackets and brooding stares, to understand his significance.

After their meteoric rise, almost exactly 10 years after Elvis' own, The Beatles asked their manager Brian Epstein to set up a meeting. He, in turn, contacted his counterpart Colonel Parker. The meeting was set. Both parties agreed to keep it secret, but the Colonel leaked the news and at least one hundred fans showed up outside Elvis' Bel Air home on August 27, 1965.

Body guard Jerry Schilling met them at the door and they were greeted by Elvis and Pricilla. According to Priscilla, they were bashful and awkward meeting their idol, especially John Lennon, "John was shy and timid. Looking at him, I really believe that he couldn't believe he was there with Elvis Presley." Elvis told them, "Guys, if you are just going to stand around and stare at me I might as well do my own thing" and he grabbed a bass guitar and they finally relaxed. "It was one of the great meetings of my life," McCartney would later recall. Sadly, there are no photos of the meeting.

Three years later, when The Beatles recorded "Lady Madonna," Ringo would say of McCartney's vocal, "It sounds like Elvis, doesn't it? No, it doesn't sound like Elvis... it IS Elvis." Elvis, in turn, would do live covers of Beatles songs, "Something," "Get Back," "Hey Jude," "Yesterday," and his own version of "Lady Madonna," perhaps acknowledging their tribute.

However, Elvis would turn on The Beatles during his meeting with President Nixon in 1970, telling him he thought they posed a threat to the nation. Still, he would meet George Harrison backstage at Madison Square Garden a few years later and they shook hands. Harrison was dressed in jeans with his hair long ("I was like a hippy") and Elvis was in full jumpsuit regalia. Harrison recalled, "He did a couple of good tunes...but he was great when he was great."

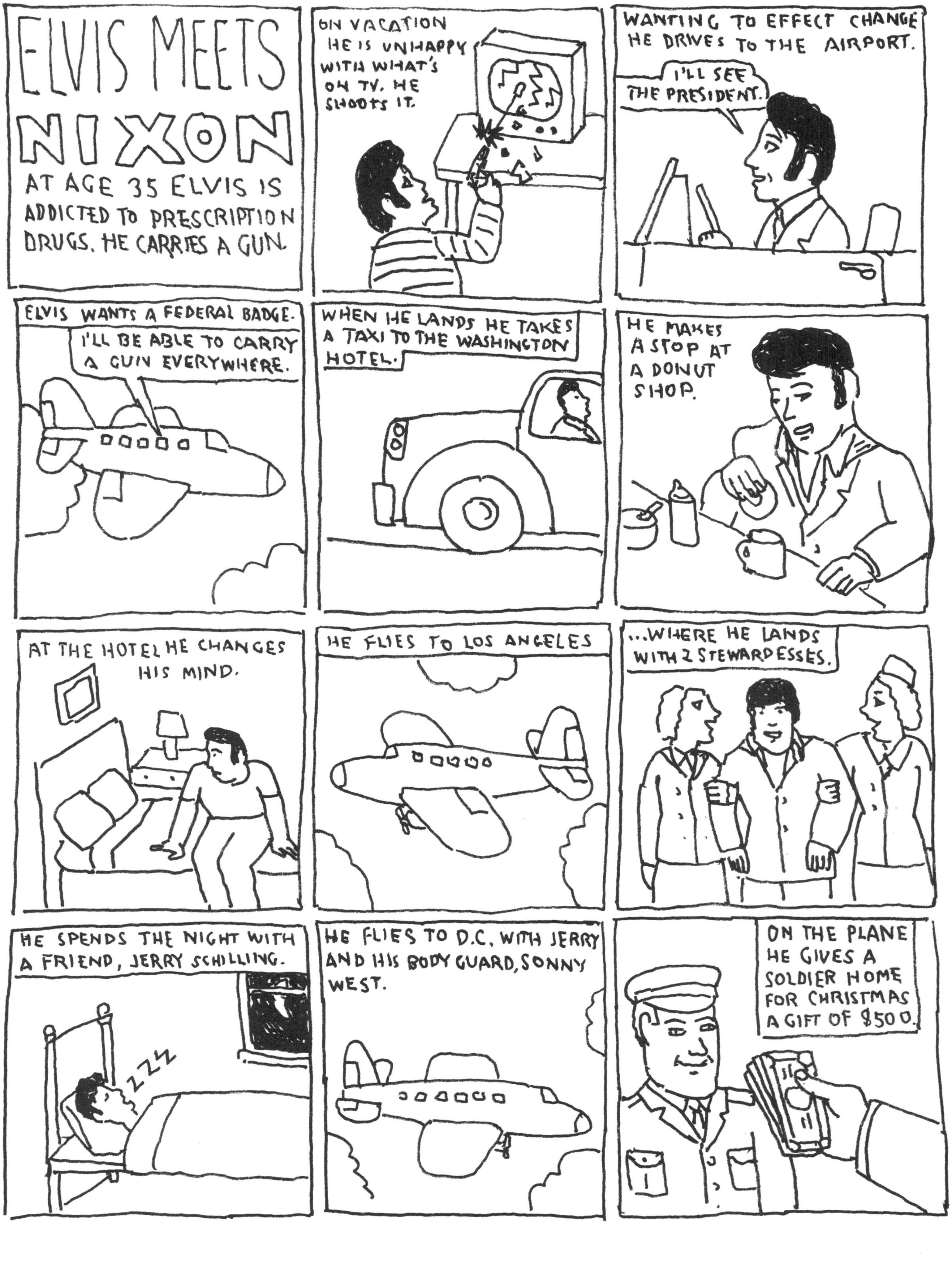
ELVIS MEETS NIXON
AT AGE 35 ELVIS IS ADDICTED TO PRESCRIPTION DRUGS. HE CARRIES A GUN.
ON VACATION HE IS UNHAPPY WITH WHAT'S ON TV. HE SHOOTS IT.
WANTING TO EFFECT CHANGE HE DRIVES TO THE AIRPORT.
I'LL SEE THE PRESIDENT.
ELVIS WANTS A FEDERAL BADGE.
I'LL BE ABLE TO CARRY A GUN EVERYWHERE.
WHEN HE LANDS HE TAKES A TAXI TO THE WASHINGTON HOTEL.
HE MAKES A STOP AT A DONUT SHOP.
AT THE HOTEL HE CHANGES HIS MIND.
HE FLIES TO LOS ANGELES
...WHERE HE LANDS WITH 2 STEWARDESSES.
HE SPENDS THE NIGHT WITH A FRIEND, JERRY SCHILLING.
ZZZ
HE FLIES TO D.C. WITH JERRY AND HIS BODY GUARD, SONNY WEST.
ON THE PLANE HE GIVES A SOLDIER HOME FOR CHRISTMAS A GIFT OF $500.

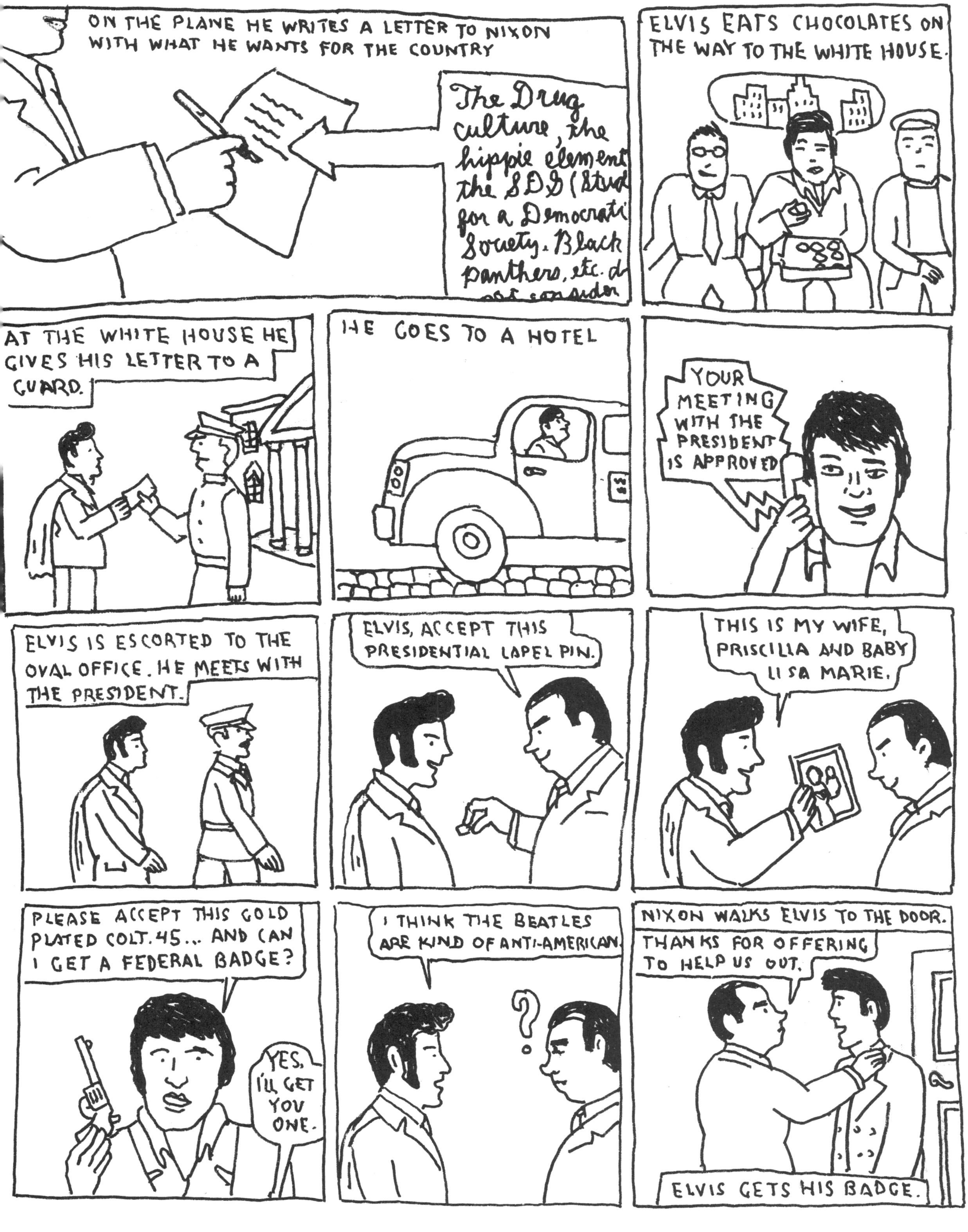
ON THE PLANE HE WRITES A LETTER TO NIXON WITH WHAT HE WANTS FOR THE COUNTRY
The Drug culture, the hippie element the SDS (Stud for a Democrati Society, Black panthers, etc. d
ELVIS EATS CHOCOLATES ON THE WAY TO THE WHITE HOUSE.
AT THE WHITE HOUSE HE GIVES HIS LETTER TO A GUARD.
HE GOES TO A HOTEL
YOUR MEETING WITH THE PRESIDENT IS APPROVED
ELVIS IS ESCORTED TO THE OVAL OFFICE. HE MEETS WITH THE PRESIDENT.
ELVIS, ACCEPT THIS PRESIDENTIAL LAPEL PIN.
THIS IS MY WIFE, PRISCILLA AND BABY LISA MARIE.
PLEASE ACCEPT THIS GOLD PLATED COLT.45... AND CAN I GET A FEDERAL BADGE?
YES, I'LL GET YOU ONE.
I THINK THE BEATLES ARE KIND OF ANTI-AMERICAN.
?
NIXON WALKS ELVIS TO THE DOOR.
THANKS FOR OFFERING TO HELP US OUT.
ELVIS GETS HIS BADGE.

What He Wore

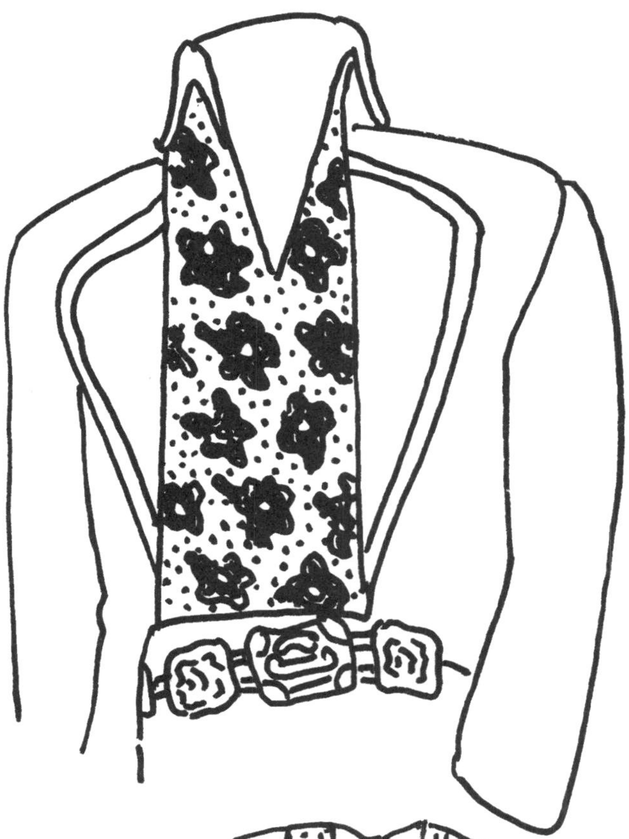

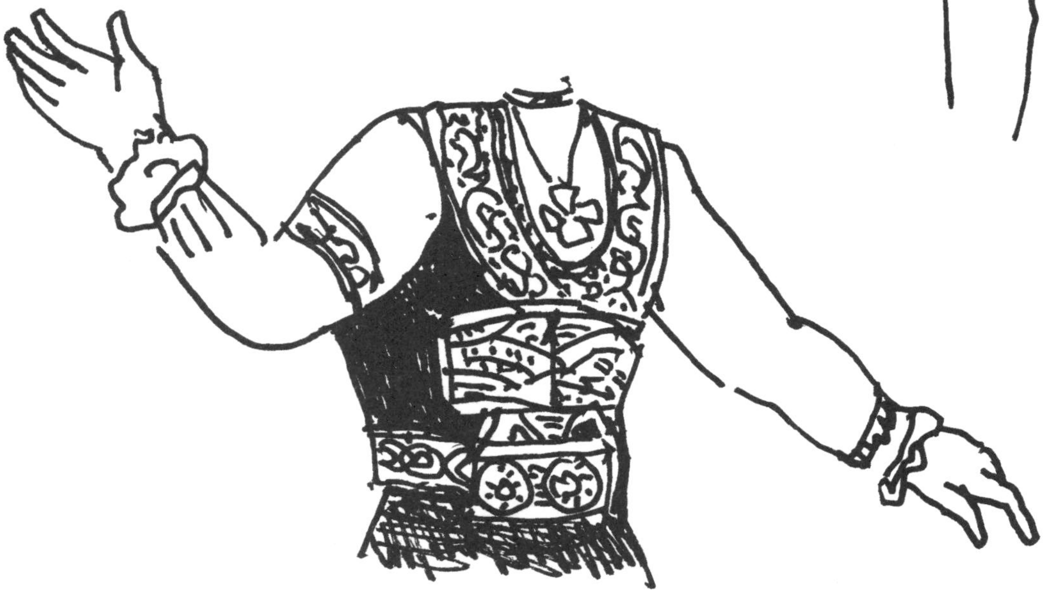

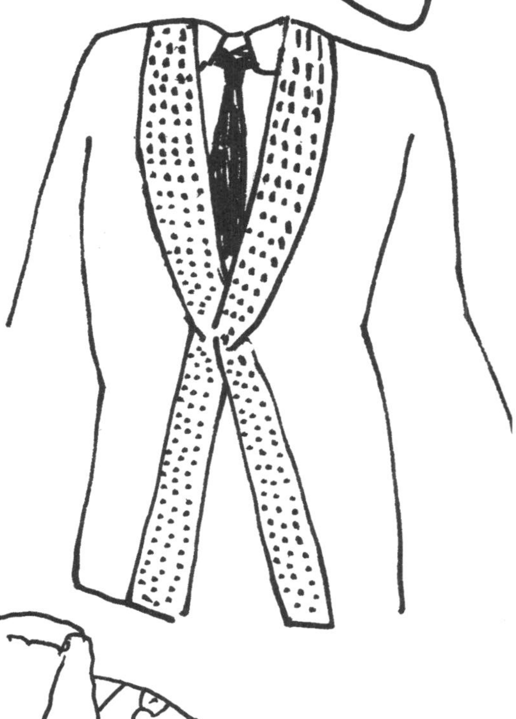

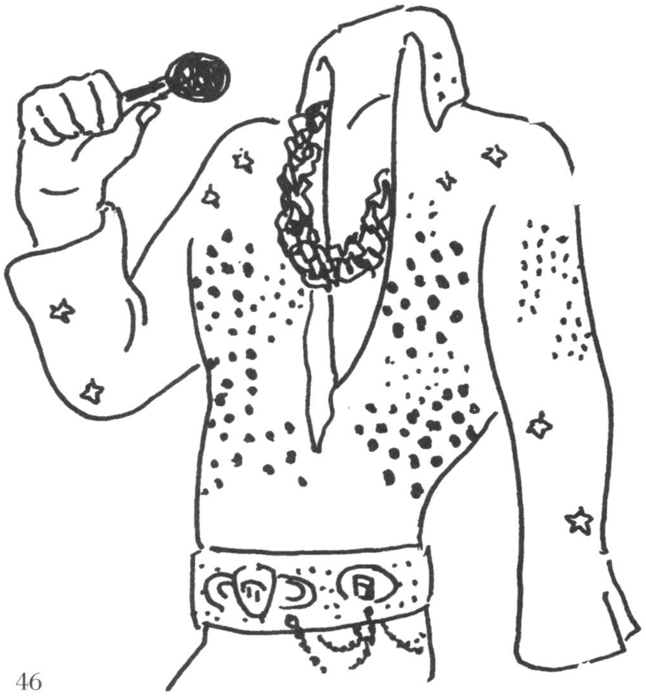

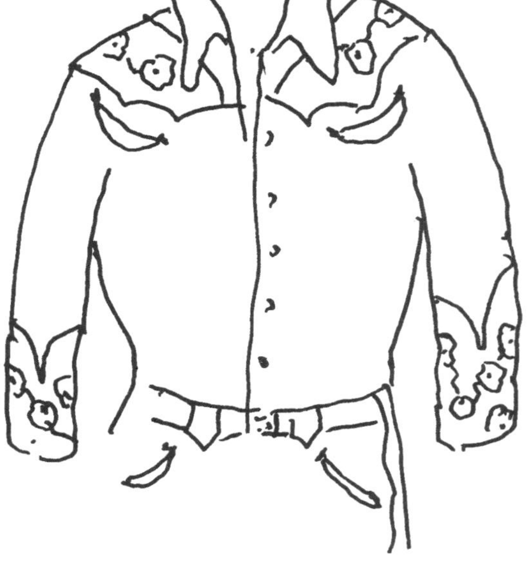

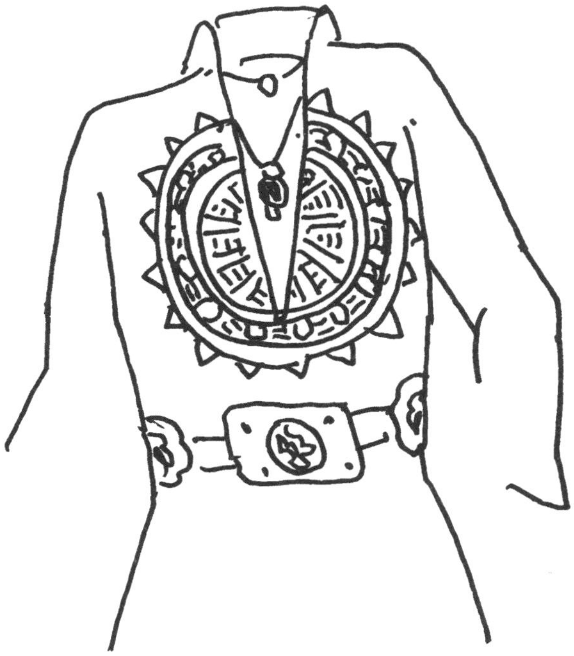

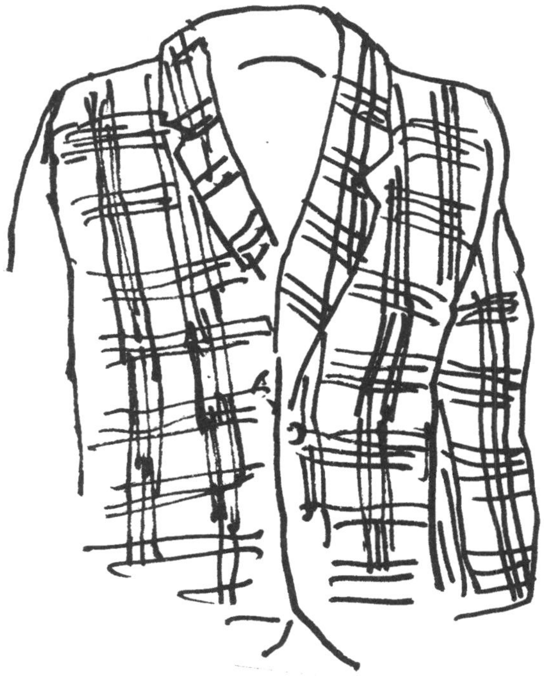

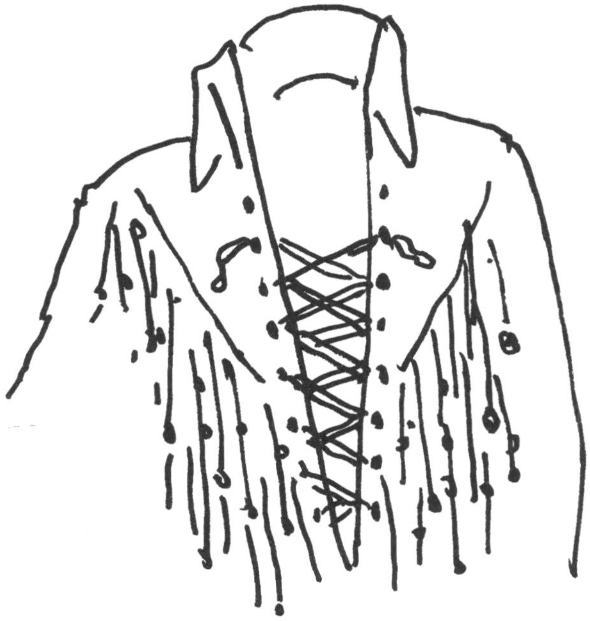

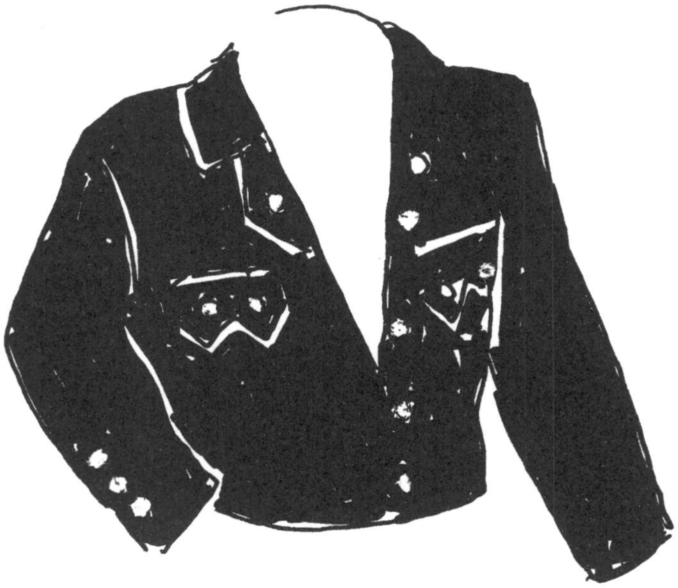

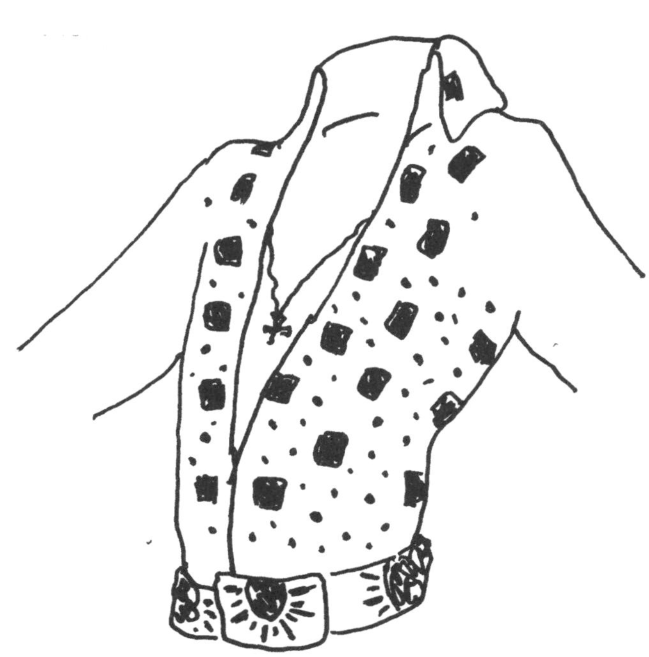

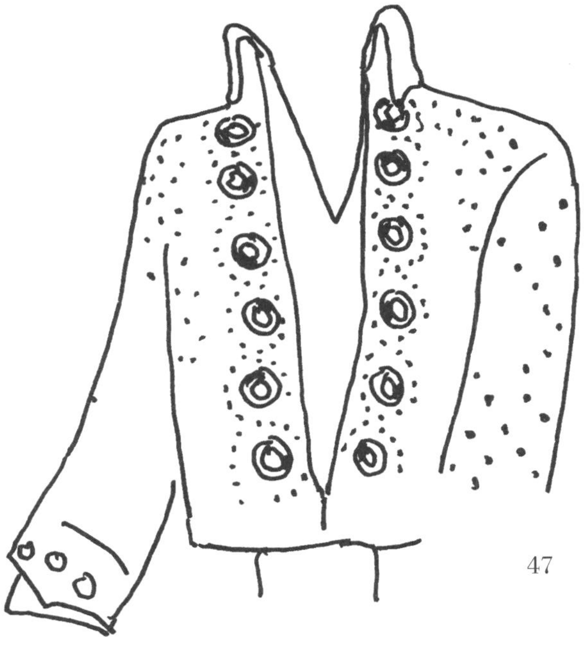

Hair

Where did Elvis' hairstyle come from? Elvis' natural hair color was sandy blond. Prior to hitting the national scene, he dyed it jet back, something he would maintain through his life, and combed it into a pompadour. He used Miss Clairol 51 D and sometimes shoe polish when dying it himself, and even dyed his eyelashes. While the most obvious influences of this look were his film idols Dean Martin and Tony Curtis (who also dyed his hair black for certain roles), the roots of this style may go back further.

As a child, Elvis was an avid reader of comic books, particularly those featuring the teenage superhero Captain Marvel Jr. He had made his appearance in 1941. Elvis was a big fan of the medium. "When I was a child, I was a dreamer. I read comic books, and I was the hero of the comic book." With his shiny jet black hair combed high, with a single ducktail curl on his forehead, the comic book character appears to have set the style for Presley in years to come. Elvis' collection of Captain Marvel Jr. comic books is kept at Graceland and a copy of Captain Marvel Jr. #51 (1947) is on display at his childhood home at Memphis' Lauderdale Courts housing complex. Elvis once confided to his cousin Earl, "I believe there's a Superboy inside me, just waiting to bust out."

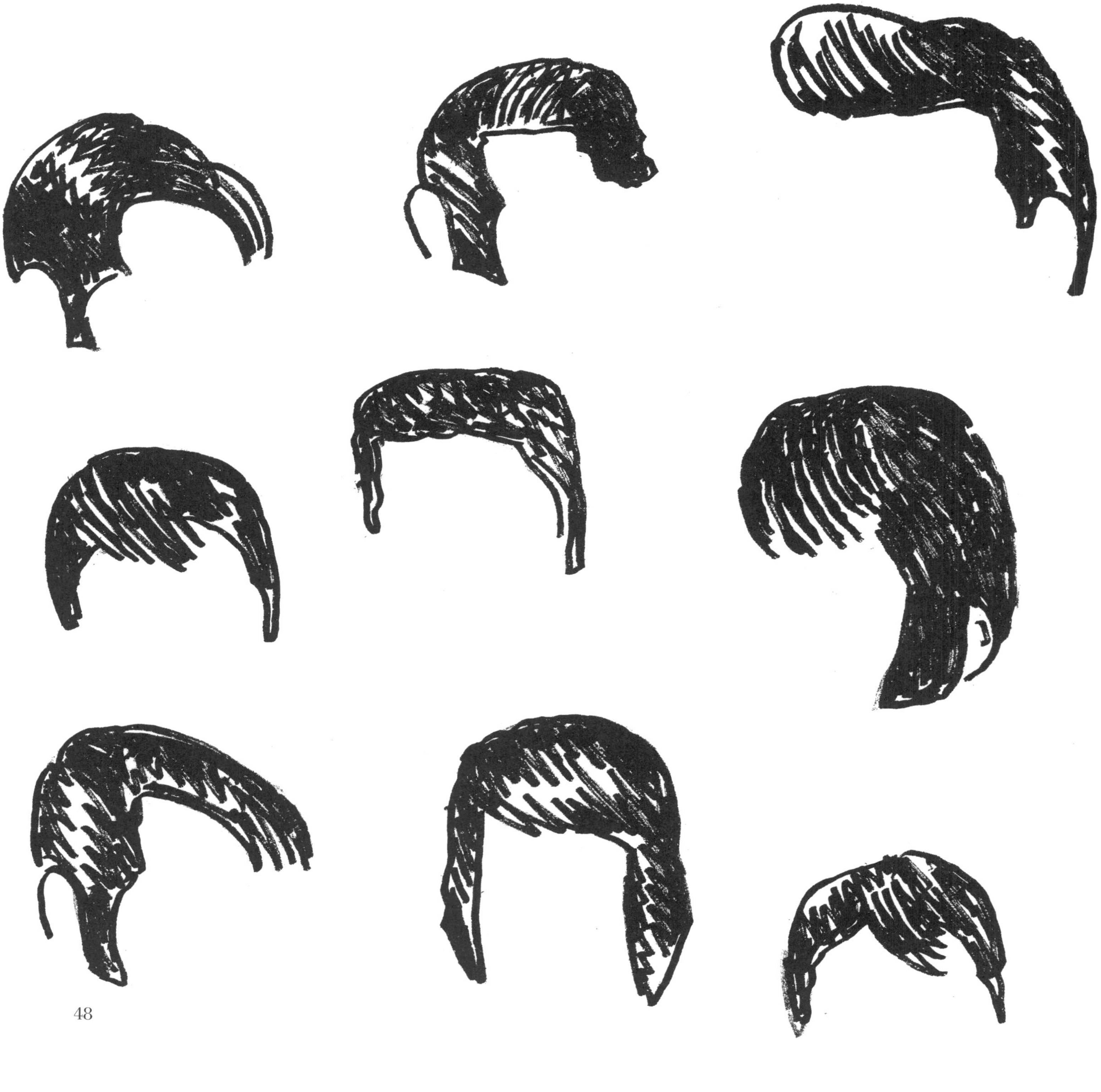

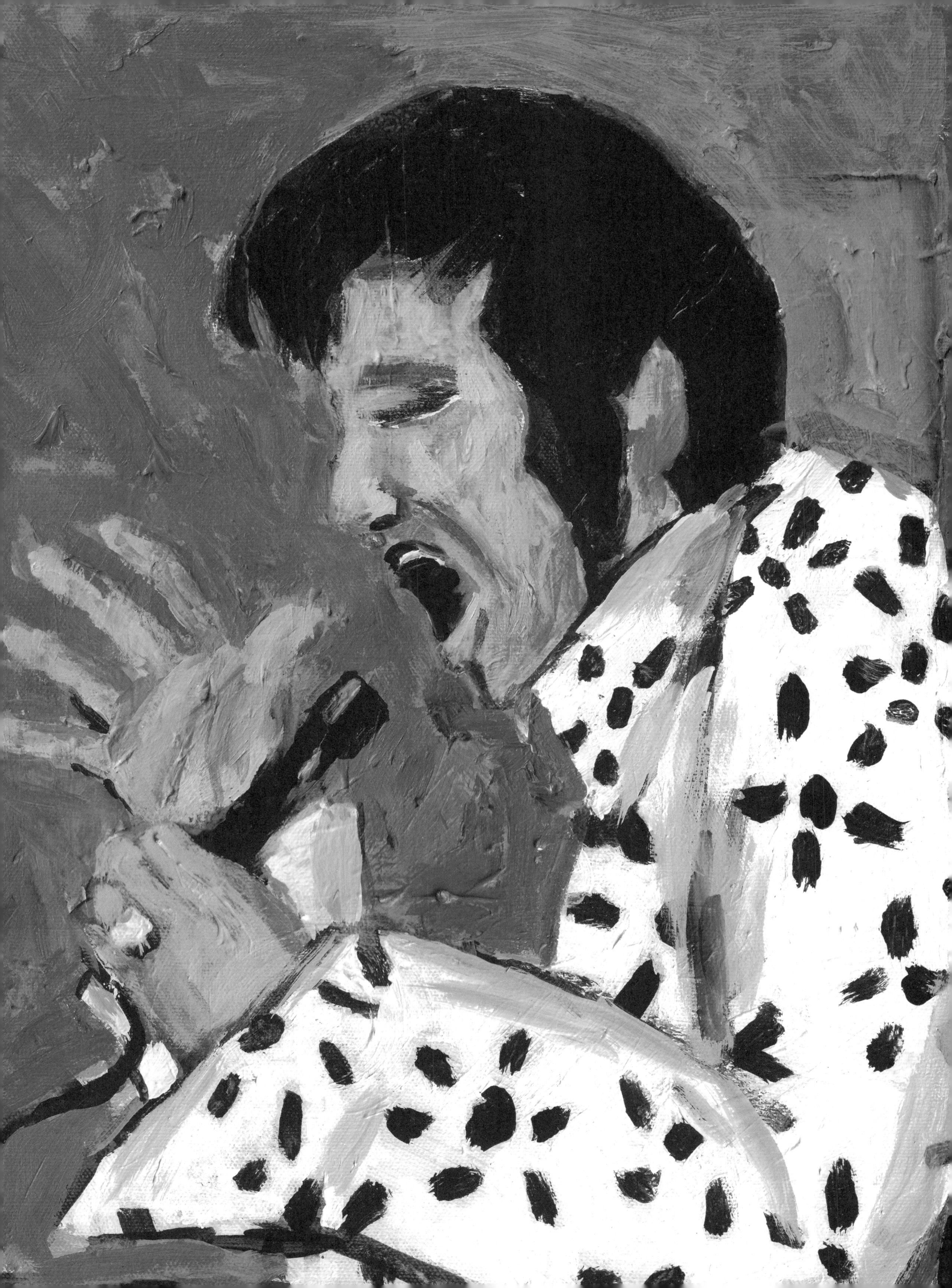

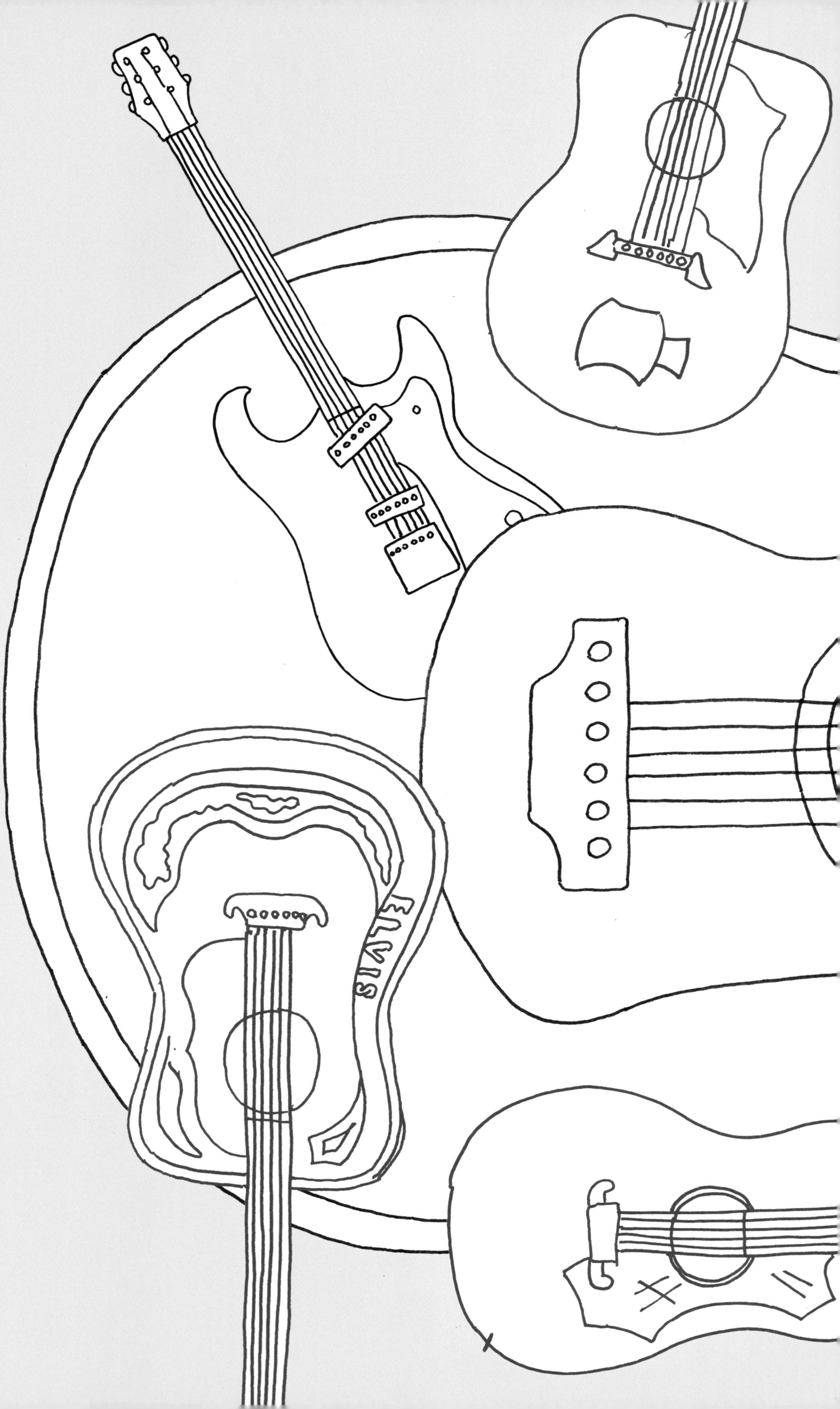
ELVIS

Guitars

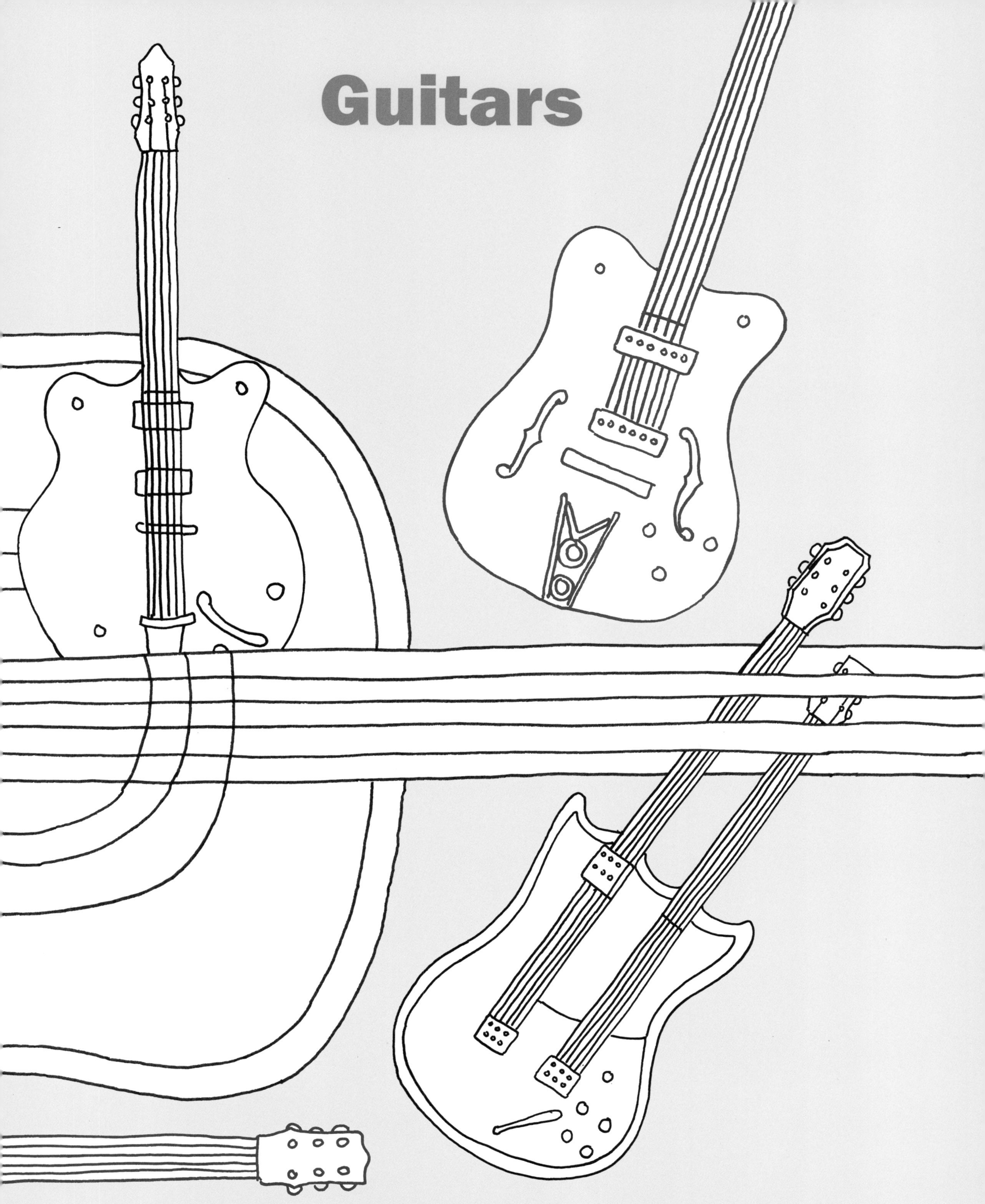

Songs

Too Much (1957)
Surrender (1961)
I Want You, I Need You, I Love You (1956)
Don't (1958)
Rock-A-Hula Baby (1961)
A Fool Such as I (1959)
A Big Hunk O' Love (1959)
Hard Headed Woman (1958)
Guitar Man (1968)
Love Me Tender (1956)
Are You Lonesome Tonight (1960)
Heartbreak Hotel (1956)
Can't Help Falling in Love (1961)

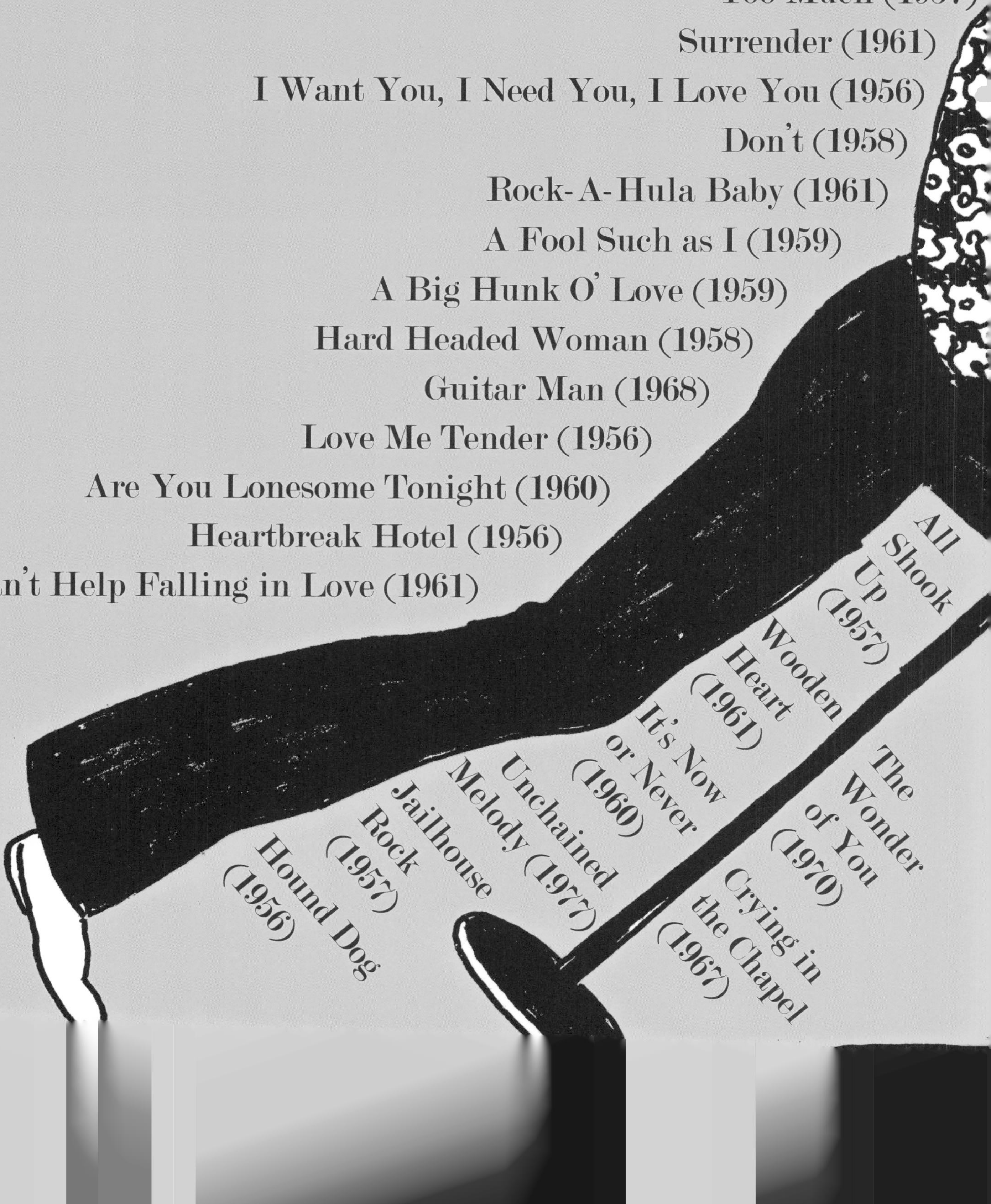

All Shook Up (1957)
Wooden Heart (1961)
It's Now or Never (1960)
Unchained Melody (1977)
Jailhouse Rock (1957)
Hound Dog (1956)
The Wonder of You (1970)
Crying in the Chapel (1967)

Stuck on You (1960)
If I Can Dream (1968)
She's Not You (1962)
Always on my Mind (1973)
Good Luck Charm (1962)
I Forgot to Remember to Forget (1956)
Return to Sender (1962)
Suspicious Minds (1969)
Blue Christmas (1957)
Don't Be Cruel (1956)
Moody Blue (1977)

Tours

NIIHAU
KAUAI
OAHU
HONOlulu
HAWA
HAWAII
Hilo

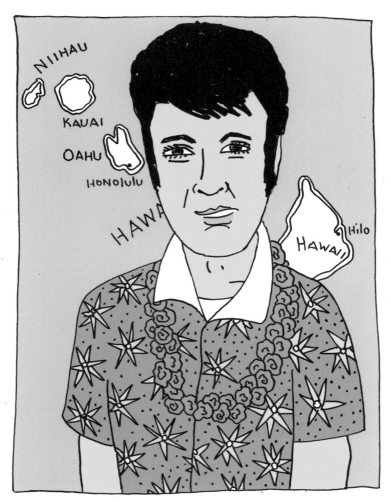

Elvis would hit the stage again regularly after his televised "Comeback Special" in 1968. In comparison to his earlier days, his touring band now included two gospel groups, The Imperials and The Sweet Inspirations, a horn and string section, piano, rhythm guitar and drums, led by lead guitarist James Burton. When performing, he dressed in high-collared bejeweled jumpsuits and performed karate moves as part of his new repertoire. This would remain his onstage persona right through his last performances in 1977.

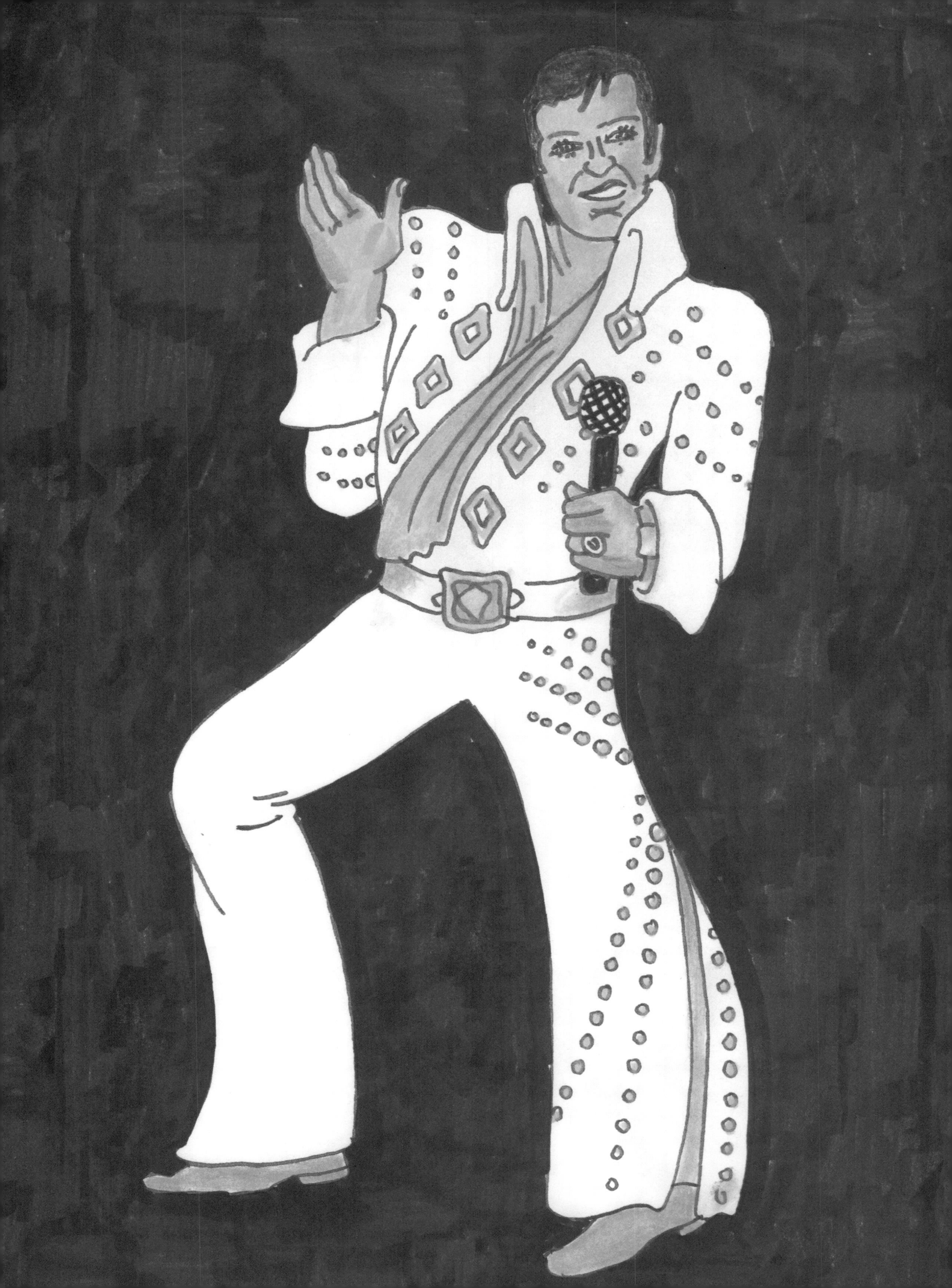

Priscilla

While stationed in Germany, a 24-year old Elvis met 14-year-old Priscilla Beaulieu. Not wishing to follow in the footsteps of fellow rocker Jerry Lee Lewis who married his 13-year old cousin, causing a great scandal in 1958, Elvis conveyed his proper intentions to her adoptive father. "Well, sir, I happen to be very fond of her. She's a lot more mature than her age... I guess you might say I need someone to talk to." Cilia, as he called her, would later recall, "Blinded by love, I saw none of his faults or weaknesses. He was to become the passion of my life."

They spent long hours into the evening talking. Elvis' mother died soon after that initial meeting and they discussed his loss. He also talked about his fear that fans were forgetting him back home. In 1960, after his discharge, Presley returned home to Graceland. Six months later, he sent for Priscilla to visit. Three years later, Priscilla convinced her parents that she should move to Memphis permanently and finish high school there. Cilia moved into Graceland. "He taught me everything: how to dress, walk, apply makeup and wear my hair, how to return love—his way." She dyed

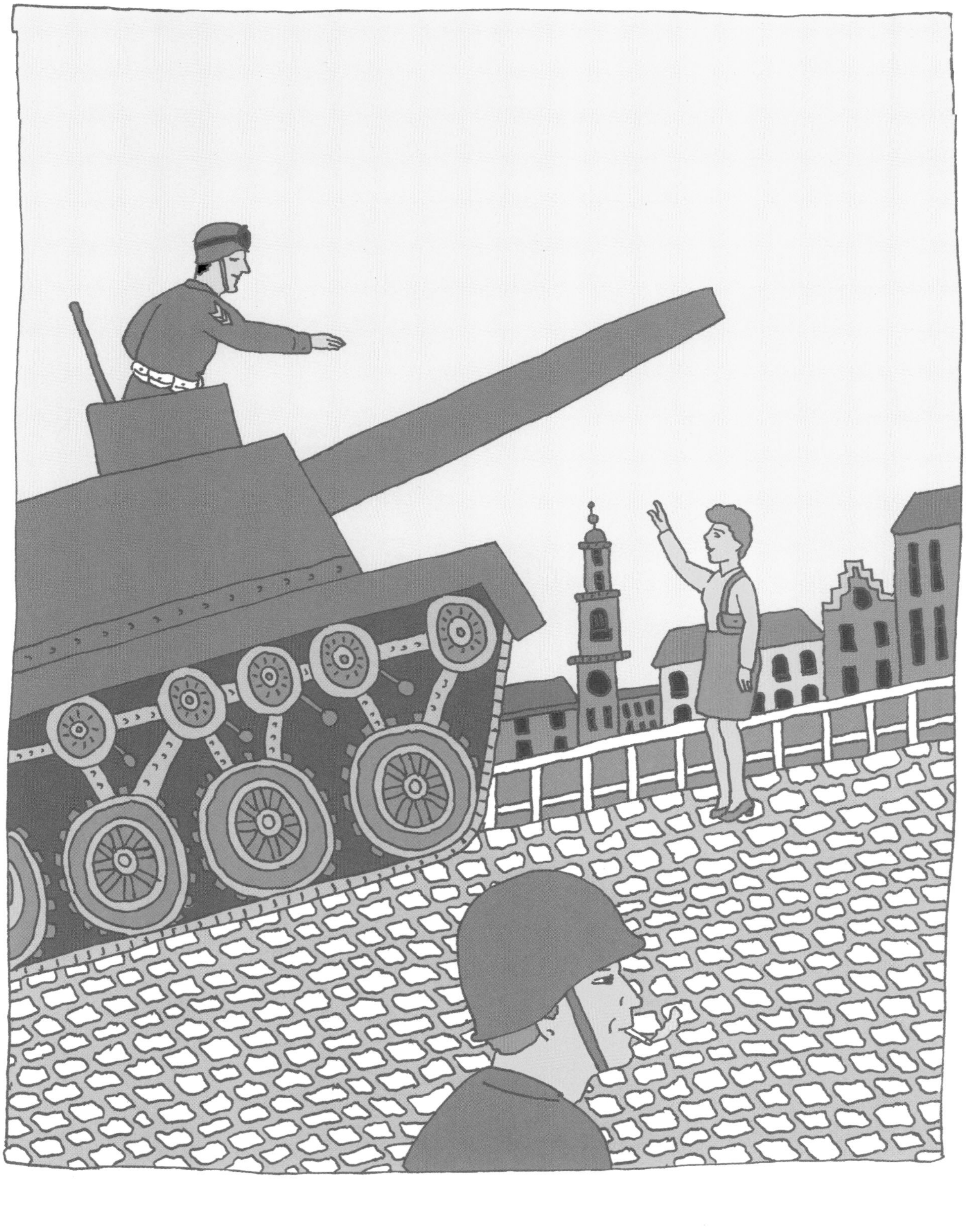

her hair jet black, just like Elvis. Also like him she started taking amphetamines and sleeping pills but, unlike him, quit.

They would eventually marry in 1966, when she was 22-years old, after a seven-and-a-half-year courtship. The wedding took place in The Aladdin Hotel in Las Vegas. Elvis put a 3½-carat diamond ring on her finger and carried her over the threshold singing "The Hawaiian Wedding Song."

Nine months later Lisa Marie was born. She was his only child and he was devoted to her.

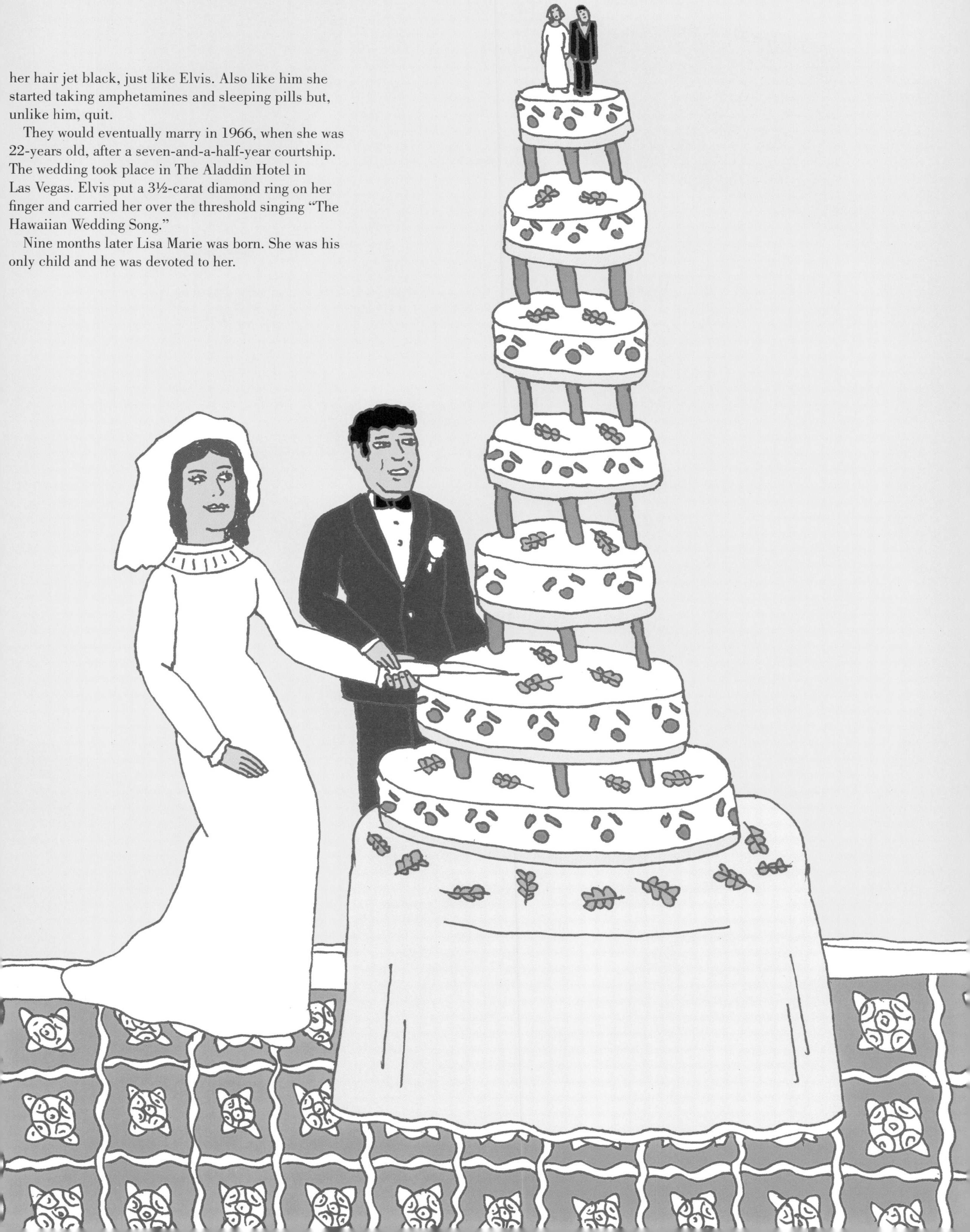

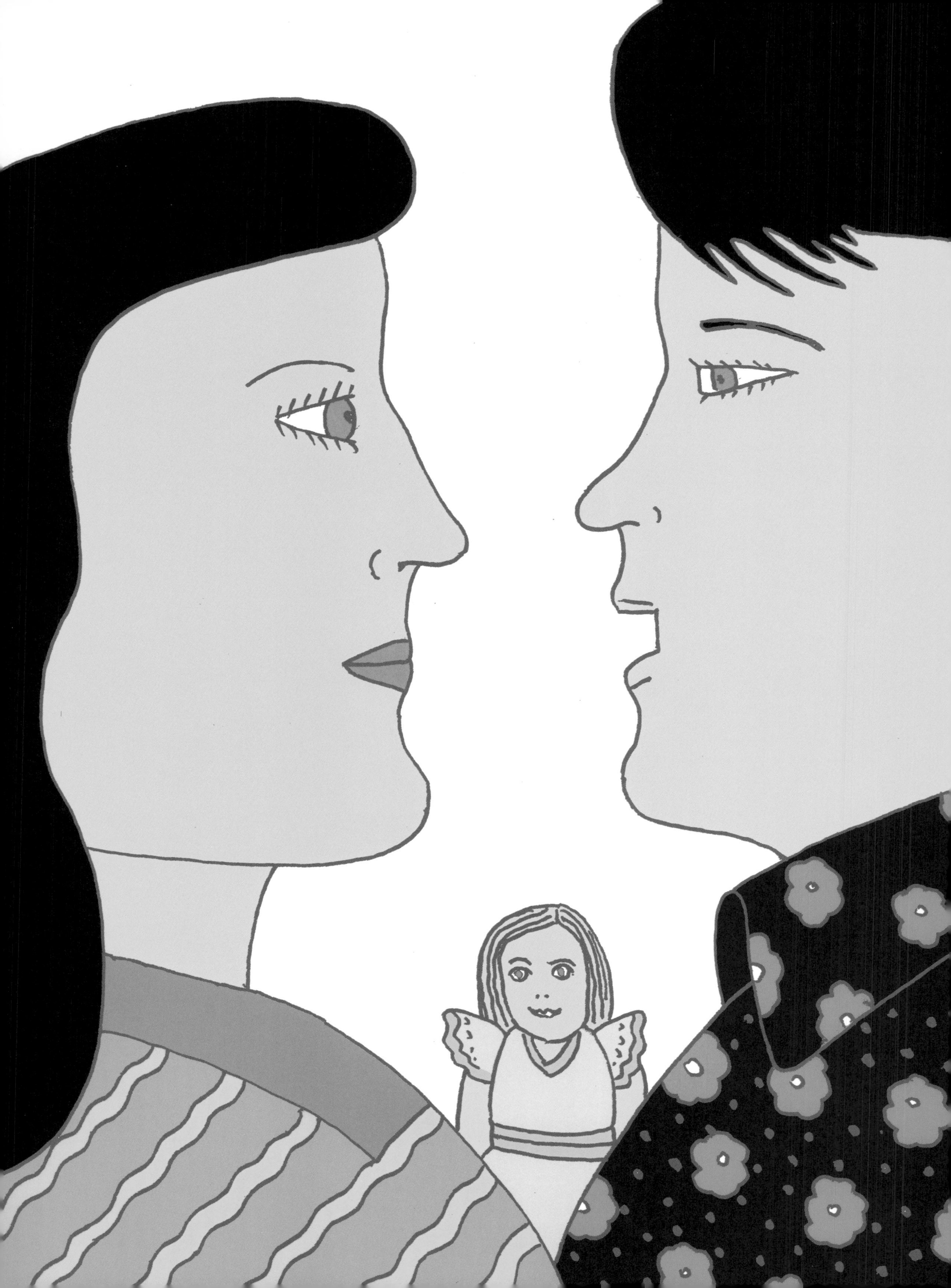

Divorce

On January 14, 1973, Elvis made television and entertainment history with his live via satellite special *Elvis: Aloha from Hawaii*, broadcast to nearly 40 countries throughout Asia, Europe, and the rest of the world (but not to the United States where it was delayed until March due to Super Bowl VII). That same year his New Year's Eve Show in Pontiac, Michigan, grossed over $800,000, the largest sum ever brought in by a single artist in a one night appearance.

Things at home were not as good. Priscilla and Elvis separated in 1972, and his new girlfriend, one-time Memphis beauty queen Linda Thompson, moved in to Graceland. In August of that year the Presleys filed for divorce. During a press conference, a reporter asked Elvis whether or not he was satisfied with his image. Presley replied, "Well, the human being is one thing. The image is another. It's very hard to live up to an image." The Presley's divorce took effect on October 9, 1973.

Drugs

He overdosed twice that same year on barbiturates. Despite failing health, he continued his intensive touring schedule.

Final Days

By 1976, Elvis was experiencing financial woes and his
father, Vernon, fired several of the "Memphis Mafia"
who had been with him for years. That same year he
and Thompson split up, and he took up with a new
girlfriend, Ginger Alden. Elvis began to noticeably gain
weight, which resulted in splitting his pants on stage
during one of his famous karate moves. His addiction
to pharmaceuticals worsened. In 1977 he began his last
national concert tour looking sweaty and bloated. While
still occasionally in good voice, his performances are
increasingly erratic. During a filmed version of "Are You
Lonesome Tonight?" he rambles incoherently, slurring
his words. According to journalist Tony Scherman,
"Presley had become a grotesque caricature of his sleek,
energetic former self. Hugely overweight, his mind dulled
by the pharmacopoeia he daily ingested, he was barely
able to pull himself through his abbreviated concerts."
He canceled four shows, unable to get out of bed. By that
point, he suffered from multiple ailments: glaucoma, high
blood pressure, liver damage, and an enlarged colon.

On the afternoon of August 16, 1977, Elvis passed
away at Graceland, found on the bathroom floor. He was
42. 80,000 fans attended his funeral. On June 7, 1982
Graceland Mansion opened for public tours. There are
over 650,000 visitors each year.

ELVIS AARON
PRESLEY
1935
—
1977

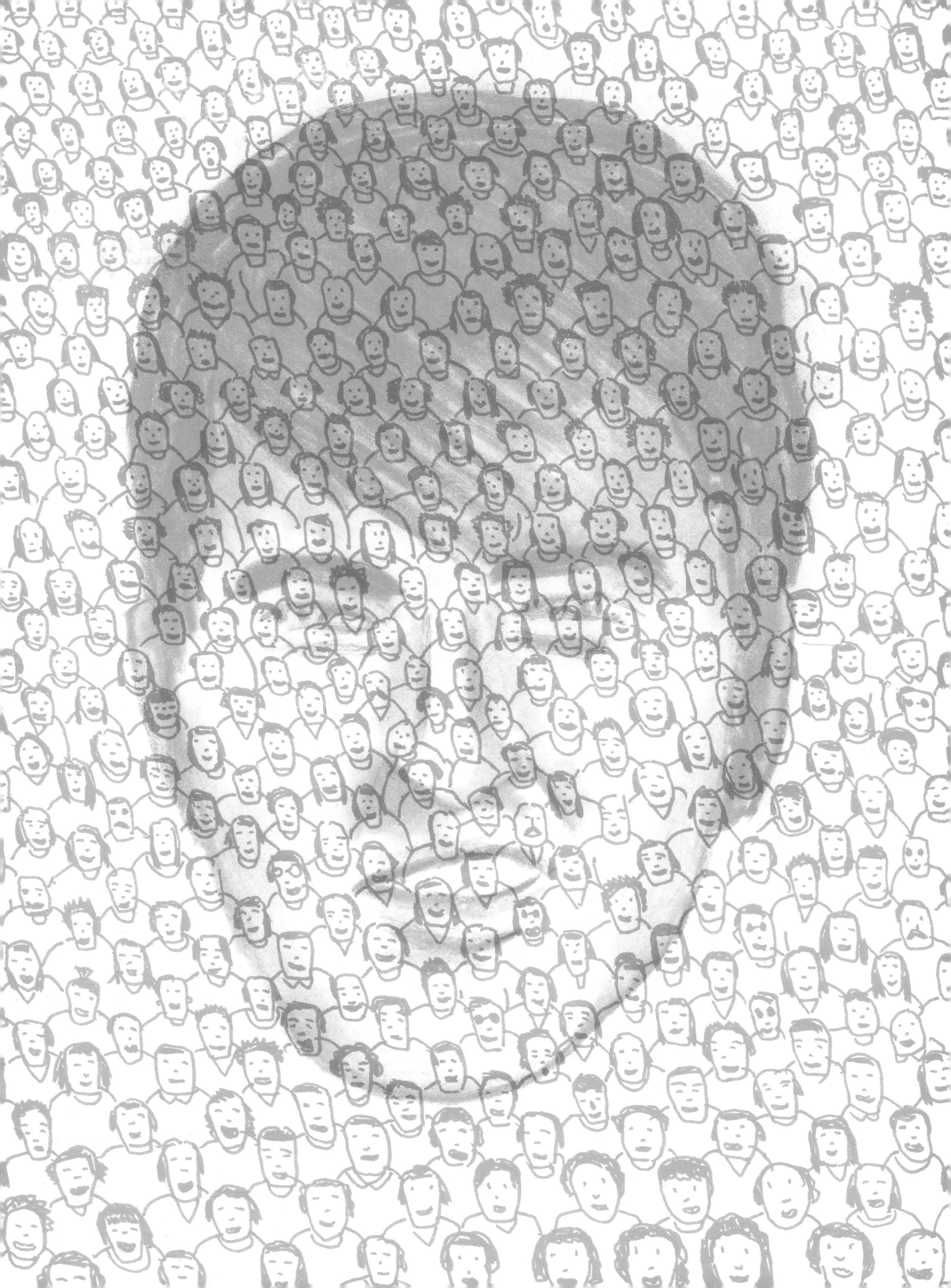

Filmography

Presley acted in a total of 31 films, from 1956 to 1969, as well as two documentaries of his tours, *Elvis: That's the Way It Is* in 1970 and *Elvis on Tour* in 1972. His leading ladies and co-stars included many big names of the day and recent past, including Barbara Stanwyck, Angela Lansbury, Juliet Prowse, Mary Tyler Moore, Joan Blondell, Ann-Margret and Lizabeth Scott, as well as Academy Award winners Burgess Meredith, Walter Matthau, among others.

1957

JAILHOUSE ROCK

Judy Tyler

1961

FOLLOW THAT DREAM

Anne Helm

1962

KID GALAHAD

Lola Albright and Gig Young

1956

LOVING YOU

Lizabeth Scott

1958

G.I. BLUES

Juliet Prowse

1961

BLUE HAWAII

Joan Blackman and
Angela Lansbury

1963

KISSIN' COUSINS

Glenda Farrell

1956

LOVE ME TENDER

Debra Paget

1960

WILD IN THE COUNTRY

Hope Lange and Tuesday Weld

1962

IT HAPPENED AT THE
WORLD'S FAIR

Joan O'Brien

1963

FUN IN ACAPULCO

Ursula Andress

1957

KING CREOLE

Carolyn Jones

1960

FLAMING STAR

Barbara Eden

1962

GIRLS! GIRLS! GIRLS!

Stella Stevens

1964

GIRL HAPPY

Shelley Fabares

1964

ROUSTABOUT

Barbara Stanwyck and
Joan Freeman

1965

TICKLE ME

Julie Adams

1967

STAY AWAY, JOE

Joan Blondell

1968

LIVE A LITTLE, LOVE
A LITTLE

Michele Carey

1964

VIVA LAS VEGAS

Ann-Margret

1966

EASY COME, EASY GO

Annette Day

1967

CLAMBAKE

Shelley Fabares

1968

SPEEDWAY

Nancy Sinatra

1965

FRANKIE AND JOHNNY

Donna Douglas

1966

SPINOUT

Shelley Fabares

1967

DOUBLE TROUBLE

Annette Day

1969

CHANGE OF HABIT

Mary Tyler Moore

1965

HARUM SCARUM

Mary Ann Mobley

1966

PARADISE, HAWAIIAN
STYLE

Suzanna Leigh

1968

CHARRO!

Ina Balin

1969

THE TROUBLE WITH GIRLS

Marlyn Mason

ELVIS DISCOGRAPHY

Albums

Albums

ELVIS PRESLEY
Released: March 23, 1956
Label: RCA

ELVIS
Released: October 19, 1956
Label: RCA

ELVIS' CHRISTMAS ALBUM
Released: October 15, 1957
Label: RCA

FOR LP FANS ONLY
Released: February 6, 1959
Label: RCA

A DATE WITH ELVIS
Released: July 24, 1959
Label: RCA

ELVIS IS BACK!
Released: April 8, 1960
Label: RCA

HIS HAND IN MINE
Released: November 10, 1960
Label: RCA

SOMETHING FOR EVERYBODY
Released: June 17, 1961
Label: RCA

POT LUCK
Released: June 5, 1962
Label: RCA

HOW GREAT THOU ART
Released: February 27, 1967
Label: RCA

FROM ELVIS IN MEMPHIS
Released: June 17, 1969
Label: RCA

ELVIS COUNTRY (I'm 10,000 Years Old)
Released: January 2, 1971
Label: RCA

LOVE LETTERS FROM ELVIS
Released: June 16, 1971
Label: RCA

WORLD OF CHRISTMAS
Released: October 20, 1971
Label: RCA

ELVIS NOW
Released: February 20, 1972
Label: RCA

HE TOUCHED ME
Released: April 1, 1972
Label: RCA

ELVIS (The "Fool" Album)
Released: July 1973
Label: RCA

FOR OL' TIMES SAKE
Released: October 1, 1973
Label: RCA

GOOD TIMES
Released: March 20, 1974
Label: RCA

PROMISED LAND
Released: January 8, 1975
Label: RCA

TODAY
Released: May 7, 1975
Label: RCA

FROM ELVIS PRESLEY BOULEVARD, MEMPHIS, TENNESSEE
Released: May 1, 1976
Label: RCA

MOODY BLUE
Released: July 19, 1977
Label: RCA

Soundtrack Albums

LOVING YOU
Released: July 1, 1957
Label: RCA

KING CREOLE
Released: September 19, 1958
Label: RCA

G.I. BLUES
Released: October 1, 1960
Label: RCA

BLUE HAWAII
Released: October 20, 1961
Label: RCA

GIRLS! GIRLS! GIRLS!
Released: November 9, 1962
Label: RCA

IT HAPPENED AT THE WORLD'S FAIR
Released: April 10, 1963
Label: RCA

FUN IN ACAPULCO
Released: November 1, 1963
Label: RCA

KISSIN' COUSINS
Released: April 2, 1964
Label: RCA

ROUSTABOUT
Released: October 20, 1964
Label: RCA

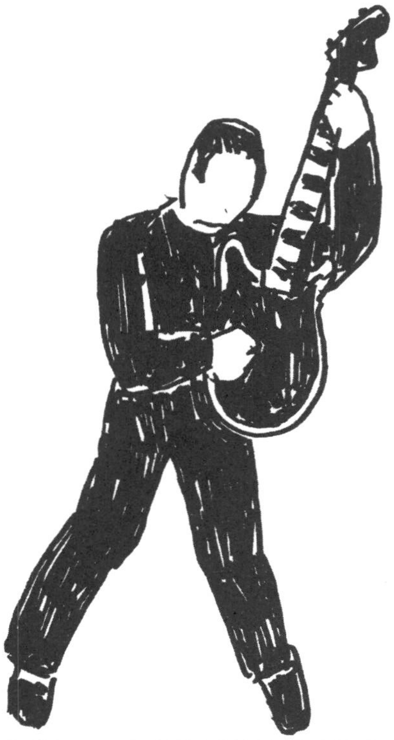

GIRL HAPPY
Released: March 2, 1965
Label: RCA

HARUM SCARUM
Released: November 3, 1965
Label: RCA

FRANKIE AND JOHNNY
Released: March 1, 1966
Label: RCA

PARADISE, HAWAIIAN STYLE
Released: June 10, 1966
Label: RCA

SPINOUT
Released: October 31, 1966
Label: RCA

DOUBLE TROUBLE
Released: June 1, 1967
Label: RCA

CLAMBAKE
Released: October 10, 1967
Label: RCA

SPEEDWAY
Released: May 1, 1968
Label: RCA

ELVIS (NBC TV Special)
Released: November 22, 1968
Label: RCA

THAT'S THE WAY IT IS
Released: November 11, 1970
Label: RCA

VIVA ELVIS
Released: November 11, 2010
Label: RCA

Live Albums

FROM MEMPHIS TO VEGAS/FROM VEGAS TO MEMPHIS
Released: October 14, 1969
Label: RCA

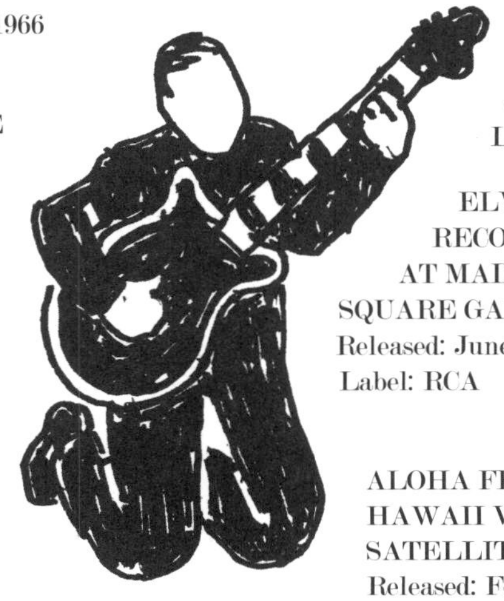

ON STAGE
Released: June 1970
Label: RCA

ELVIS: AS RECORDED AT MADISON SQUARE GARDEN
Released: June 18, 1972
Label: RCA

ALOHA FROM HAWAII VIA SATELLITE
Released: February 4, 1973
Label: RCA

ELVIS RECORDED LIVE ON STAGE IN MEMPHIS
Released: July 7, 1974
Label: RCA

ELVIS IN CONCERT
Released: October 3, 1977
Label: RCA

Spoken Word Albums

ELVIS SAILS
Released: March 1959
Label: RCA

HAVING FUN WITH ELVIS ON STAGE
Released: October 1974
Label: RCA

Compilation Albums

ELVIS' GOLDEN RECORDS
Released: March 21, 1958
Label: RCA

ELVIS' GOLD RECORDS, VOLUME 2
Released: November 13, 1959
Label: RCA

ELVIS' GOLDEN RECORDS VOLUME 3
Released: August 11, 1963
Label: RCA

ELVIS FOR EVERYONE!
Released: August 10, 1965
Label: RCA

ELVIS' GOLD RECORDS VOLUME 4
Released: January 2, 1968
Label: RCA

ELVIS: A LEGENDARY PERFORMER VOLUME 1
Released: January 2, 1974
Label: RCA

ELVIS' 40 GREATEST
Released: October 23, 1974
Label: RCA

ELVIS: A LEGENDARY PERFORMER VOLUME 2
Released: January 8, 1976
Label: RCA

THE SUN SESSIONS
Released: March 22, 1976
Label: RCA

BLUE CHRISTMAS
Released: 1976
Label: RCA

WELCOME TO MY WORLD
Released: March 1977
Label: RCA

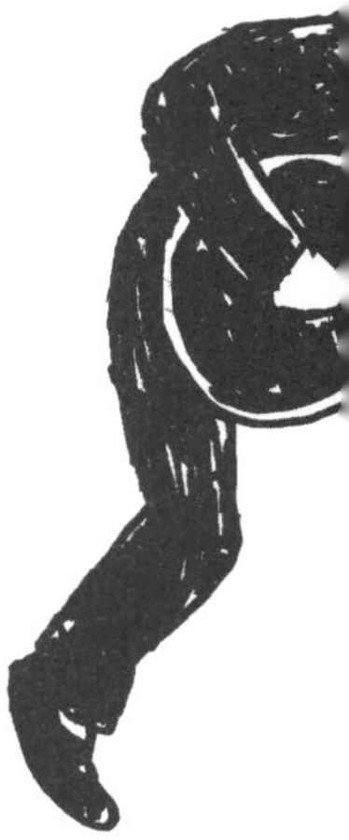

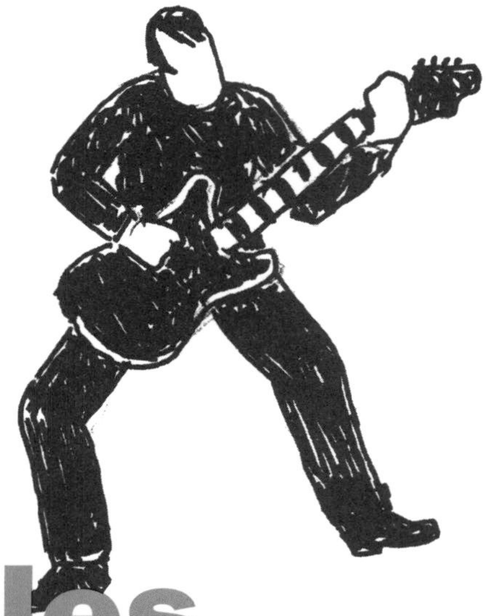

Singles

1954

That's All Right / Blue Moon of Kentucky

Good Rockin' Tonight / I Don't Care If the Sun Don't Shine

1955

You're a Heartbreaker / Milkcow Blues Boogie

Baby Let's Play House / I'm Left, You're Right, She's Gone

Mystery Train / I Forgot to Remember to Forget

1956

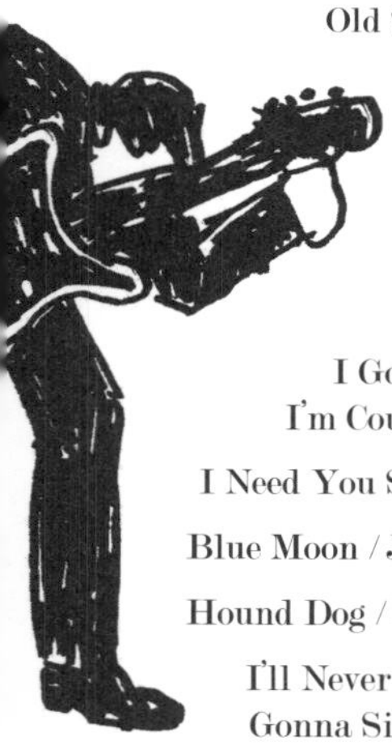

Old Shep

Money Honey

Any Way You Want Me

Tutti Frutti / Tryin' To Get To You

I Got A Woman / I'm Counting On You

I Need You So

Blue Moon / Just Because

Hound Dog / Don't Be Cruel

I'll Never Let You Go / I'm Gonna Sit Right Down And Cry (Over You)

Shake, Rattle And Roll

Love Me Tender

Blue Suede Shoes / I'm Counting On You

Elvis Presley With The Jordanaires - Blue Suede Shoes / Tutti Frutti

Heartbreak Hotel

Tryin' To Get To You / I Love You Because

Love Me Tender

I'll Never Let You Go / I'm Gonna Sit Right Down And Cry Over

My Baby Left Me

I Want You, I Need You, I Love You / My Baby Left Me

Rip It Up

1957

Peace In The Valley

Elvis Presley With The Jordanaires - Young And Beautiful / Baby I Don't Care

Mean Woman Blues / Have I Told You Lately That I Love You?

Tutti Frutti

Good Rockin' Tonight

Elvis Presley With The Jordanaires - All Shook Up / Teddy Bear

Love Me

Santa Bring My Baby Back (To Me)

Just For You

Lawdy Miss Clawdy / Tryin' To Get To You

Elvis Presley With The Jordanaires - Playing For Keeps / Too Much

My Baby Left Me

Blueberry Hill / Paralyzed

Jailhouse Rock / Treat Me Nice

All Shook Up / That's When Your Heartaches Begin

Rock 'N' Roll

Just For You

Merry Christmas

I'm Counting On You

Elvis Presley With The Jordanaires - (You're So Square) Baby I Don't Care / I Want To Be Free

1958

King Creole / Lover Doll

Dixieland Rock / Lover Doll

One Night / I Got Stung

Tutti Frutti / I Want You, I Need You, I Love You

Playing For Keeps

Elvis Presley With The Jordanaires - Hard Headed Woman / Don't Ask Me Why

Wear My Ring Around Your Neck / Doncha' Think It's Time

I'm Left, You're Right, She's Gone

Loving You

Treat Me Nice

Playing For Keeps / Too Much

How's The World Treating You / Ready Teddy

New Orleans / Lover Doll

Good Rockin' Tonight

I Got Stung / Let Me

Elvis Presley With The Jordanaires - Doncha' Think It's Time

I Need You So / Crawfish

Elvis Presley With The Jordanaires - Don't Leave Me Now / Baby I Don't Care

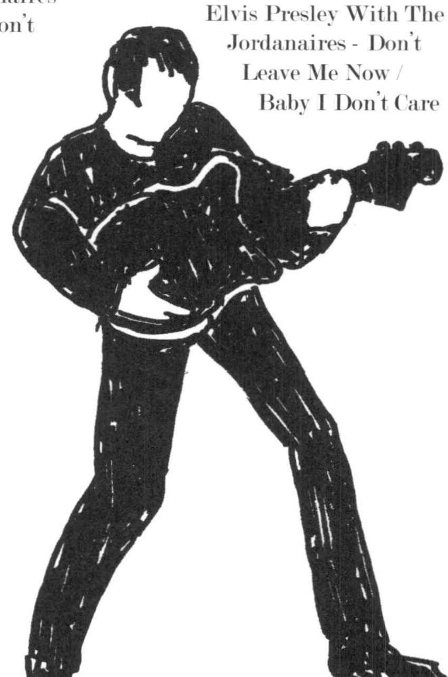

1959

Elvis Presley With The Jordanaires - A Big Hunk O' Love / My Wish Came True

Elvis Presley With The Jordanaires - I Need Your Love Tonight / A Fool Such As I

(Now and Then There's) A Fool Such as I

I Need Your Love Tonight

A Big Hunk o' Love

My Wish Came True

1960

Stuck on You

Fame and Fortune

It's Now or Never

A Mess of Blues

Are You Lonesome Tonight?

I Gotta Know

1961

Surrender

Lonely Man

Flaming Star

I Feel So Bad

Wild in the Country

(Marie's the Name) His Latest Flame

Little Sister

Can't Help Falling in Love

1962

Rock-A-Hula Baby

Good Luck Charm

Anything That's Part of You

Follow That Dream

She's Not You

Just Tell Her Jim Said Hello

King of the Whole Wide World

Return to Sender

Where Do You Come From

1963

One Broken Heart for Sale

They Remind Me Too Much of You

(You're The) Devil in Disguise/ Please Don't Drag That String Around"

Bossa Nova Baby

Witchcraft

1964

Kissin' Cousins

It Hurts Me

Kiss Me Quick

Suspicion

What'd I Say

Viva Las Vegas

Such a Night

Never Ending

Ask Me

Ain't That Loving You Baby"

Wooden Heart / Blue Christmas

1965

Do the Clam

Crying in the Chapel / I Believe in the Man in the Sky

(Such An) Easy Question

"It Feels So Right

I'm Yours

(It's a) Long Lonely Highway

Puppet on a String" / Wooden Heart

Santa Claus is Back in Town

1966

Tell Me Why

Blue River

Joshua Fit the Battle / Known Only to Him

Milky White Way / Swing Down, Sweet Chariot

Frankie and Johnny

Please Don't Stop Loving Me

Love Letters

Come What May

Spinout

All That I Am

If Every Day Was Like Christmas / How Would You Like to Be

1967

Indescribably Blue

Fools Fall in Love

Long Legged Girl (With the Short Dress On)

That's Someone You Never Forget

There's Always Me

Judy

Big Boss Man

You Don't Know Me

1968

Guitar Man

Hi-Heel Sneakers

U.S. Male

Stay Away

You'll Never Walk Alone

We Call on Him

The Critics

Notwithstanding becoming an instant national hit with America's youth Elvis was not without his critics. To many he posed a threat to their perceived chaste, conformist and comfortable decade. He began 1956 with a number one record, an appearance on the Dorsey Brothers' televised *Stage Show*, and work on his first film, *Love Me Tender*. The backlash was almost as instantaneous as his success:

"Elvis will never contribute a damn thing to music."
–Bing Crosby, 1956

"I don't want him on my show, I don't care what anyone says about him–how great a talent he is–he just won't be in my show and that's that."
–Ed Sullivan, 1956

"His performance was the most disgusting exhibition this reporter has ever seen. For Presley is the male counterpart of a hoochee-koochee dancer in a burlesque show." –*Sioux City Journal*, May 24, 1956

"Most of his action stems from the hips. In fact, devotees of the burlesque circuit will recognize his basic technique as 'grind-and-bump.' This normally is practiced by young ladies of the burlesque, but Mr. Presley has adapted it to the concert stage, with little sacrifice of its innate vulgarity."
–*Columbus Citizen*, May 27, 1956

"Mr. Presley has no discernible singing ability. His specialty is rhythm songs which he renders in an undistinguished whine; his phrasing, if it can be called that, consists of the stereotyped variations that go with a beginner's aria in a bathtub. For the ear he is an unutterable bore."
–Jack Gould, *The New York Times*, June 6, 1956

"Dreamboat Groaner Elvis ('Hi luh-huh-huh-huv-huv yew-hew') Presley."   –*Time*, June 11, 1956

"PERFORMER'S GYRATIONS MAY DOOM ROCK 'N' ROLL. The last appearance of this unspeakably untalented and vulgar young entertainer brought forth such a storm of complaints both from the press and public that I imagine any entertainer would hesitate to try him again on television."
–John Crosby, syndicated column, June 18th, 1956

"The guest performer, Elvis Presley, presented such a demonstration which was in execrable taste, bordering on obscenity. The gyrations of this young man were such an assault to the senses as to repel even the most tolerant observer."
–Harry A. Feldman, head of the music department at Bryant High School, June 18, 1956

"If he did that on the street we'd arrest him."
–California policeman, June 18, 1956

"Presley, sometimes called 'Pelvis Presley,' is a rock'n'roller whose gyrating hips have outraged music critics far and wide."
–*Charlotte Observer*, June 27, 1956

"Elvis can't sing, can't play the guitar, and can't dance. Yet two thousand idiots per show yelp every time he opens his mouth, plucks a guitar string, or shakes his pelvis like any striptease babe in town."
–Herb Rau, *Miami Daily News*, August 4, 1956

"(Popular music) has reached its lowest depths in the [grunt and groin] antics of one Elvis Presley."
–*New York Daily News*, 1956

"His kind of music is deplorable, a rancid smelling aphrodisiac...It fosters almost totally negative and destructive reactions in young people."

–Frank Sinatra, 1957

"Elvis the Pelvis hasn't any kind of singing voice."

–Hugh Thomson, *Toronto Daily Star*, 1957

"Let me admit at the outset that I don't like Elvis Presley. He's the kind of a child that other children are traditionally 'not allowed to play with.' He's a sullen, ill-kempt-looking youth. If he was my kid (and I was in a helluva lot better shape than I am), I'd smack that sneer off his face and send him out for a haircut. In all, I consider him a very distasteful individual."

–Paul Coates, *Los Angeles Mirror News*, October 31, 1957

"Elvis stays front and center, of course, muttering his lines sheepishly, and wooing Miss Tyler by collapsing like a rag doll and hooking a chin on her shoulder."

—*The New York Times*, *Jailhouse Rock* review, November 14, 1957

"The last thing you might think Elvis Presley is qualified to do, is act a diffident amateur boxer who turns out to be a tiger in the professional fight ring. And you might well persist in that opinion after seeing him in *Kid Galahad*."

–*New York Times* film critic Bosley Crowther, March 7, 1963

"This new Elvis Presley concoction is a pretty dreary effort, one that certainly won't replenish the popularity of Sir Swivel. Presley needs—and merits—more substantial material than this if his career is to continue to flourish as in the past. A few more like this and Cuhnel Parker may have to press the panic button."

–*Variety*, *Kissin' Cousins* review, March 4, 1964

"Elvis Presley had better watch his step after *Tickle Me*, his latest color musical film. This is the silliest, feeblest and dullest vehicle for the Memphis Wonder in a long time. And both Elvis and his sponsors, this time Allied Artists, should know better. In such trim packages as *Viva Las Vegas* and *Fun in Acapulco*, the Presley formula—colorful settings, tunes and pretty girls aplenty—took on real, tasty sparkle. But yesterday's flapdoodle, even weaker than the preceding *Girl Happy*, should strain the indulgence of the most ardent Presley fans. See for yourself, girls. It looks made up as it goes along." –Howard Thompson, *New York Times*, 1965

"Mr. Presley wanders through the improbable whimsies of *Harum Scarum* with all the animation of a man under deep sedation, but then he had read the script."

–Vincent Canby, *The New York Times*, December 16, 1965

"[Elvis] injected movements of the tongue and indulged in wordless singing that were singularly distasteful."
–Jack Gould, *The New York Times*, September 16, 1956

"BEWARE ELVIS PRESLEY. If the agencies (TV and other) would stop handling such nauseating stuff, all the Presleys of our land would soon be swallowed up in the oblivion they deserve."

–*America* (a Catholic weekly), 1956

"Elvis achieved a new low in spiritual degeneracy."
–Baptist minister

"Appraising Presley as an actor, he ain't. Not that it makes much difference. The presence of Presley apparently is enough to satisfy the juve set."

–*Variety*, *Love Me Tender* review, 1956

Elvis Speaks

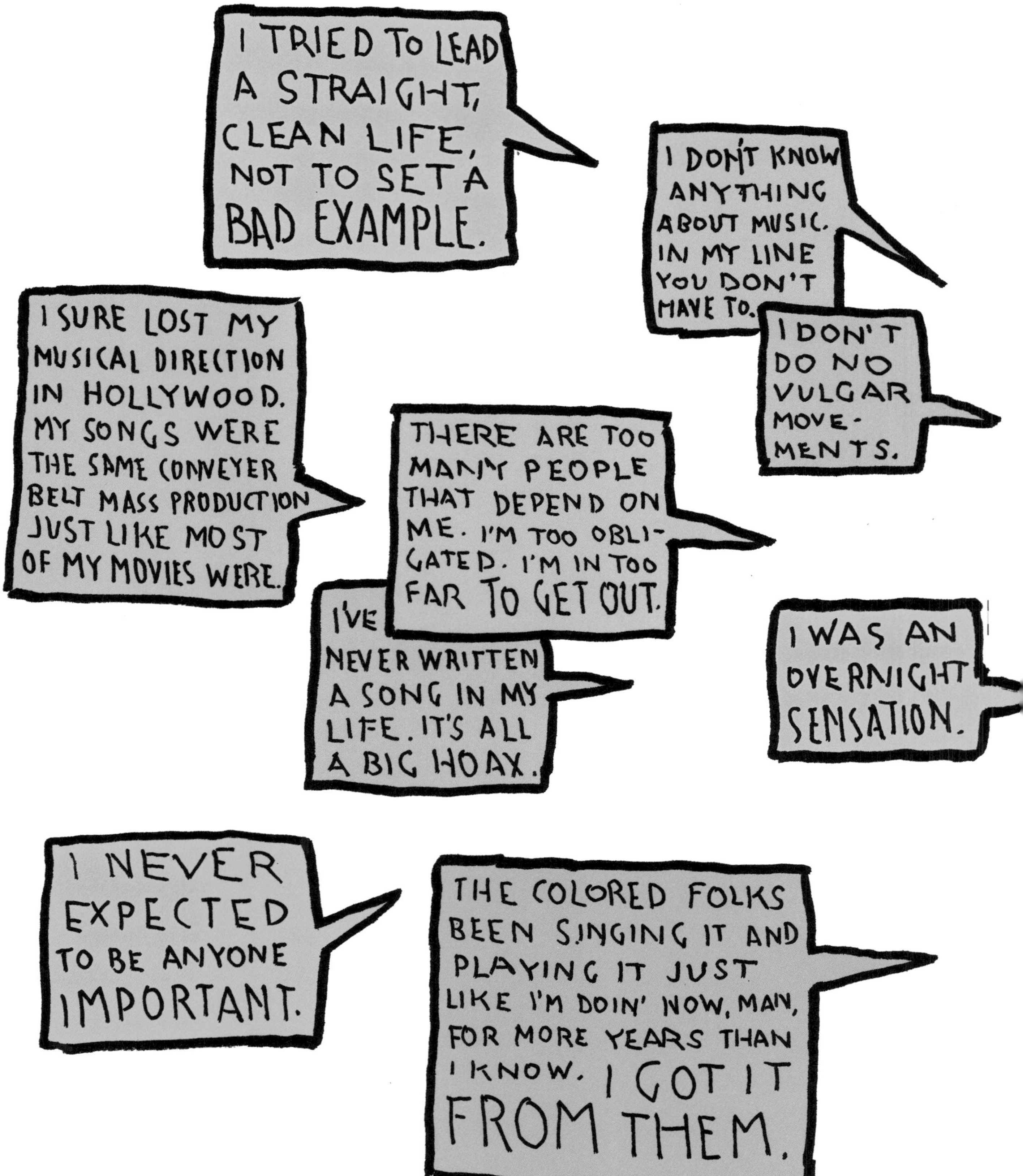
I TRIED TO LEAD A STRAIGHT, CLEAN LIFE, NOT TO SET A BAD EXAMPLE.
I DON'T KNOW ANYTHING ABOUT MUSIC. IN MY LINE YOU DON'T HAVE TO.
I DON'T DO NO VULGAR MOVE-MENTS.
I SURE LOST MY MUSICAL DIRECTION IN HOLLYWOOD. MY SONGS WERE THE SAME CONVEYER BELT MASS PRODUCTION JUST LIKE MOST OF MY MOVIES WERE.
THERE ARE TOO MANY PEOPLE THAT DEPEND ON ME. I'M TOO OBLI-GATED. I'M IN TOO FAR TO GET OUT.
I'VE NEVER WRITTEN A SONG IN MY LIFE. IT'S ALL A BIG HOAX.
I WAS AN OVERNIGHT SENSATION.
I NEVER EXPECTED TO BE ANYONE IMPORTANT.
THE COLORED FOLKS BEEN SINGING IT AND PLAYING IT JUST LIKE I'M DOIN' NOW, MAN, FOR MORE YEARS THAN I KNOW. I GOT IT FROM THEM.

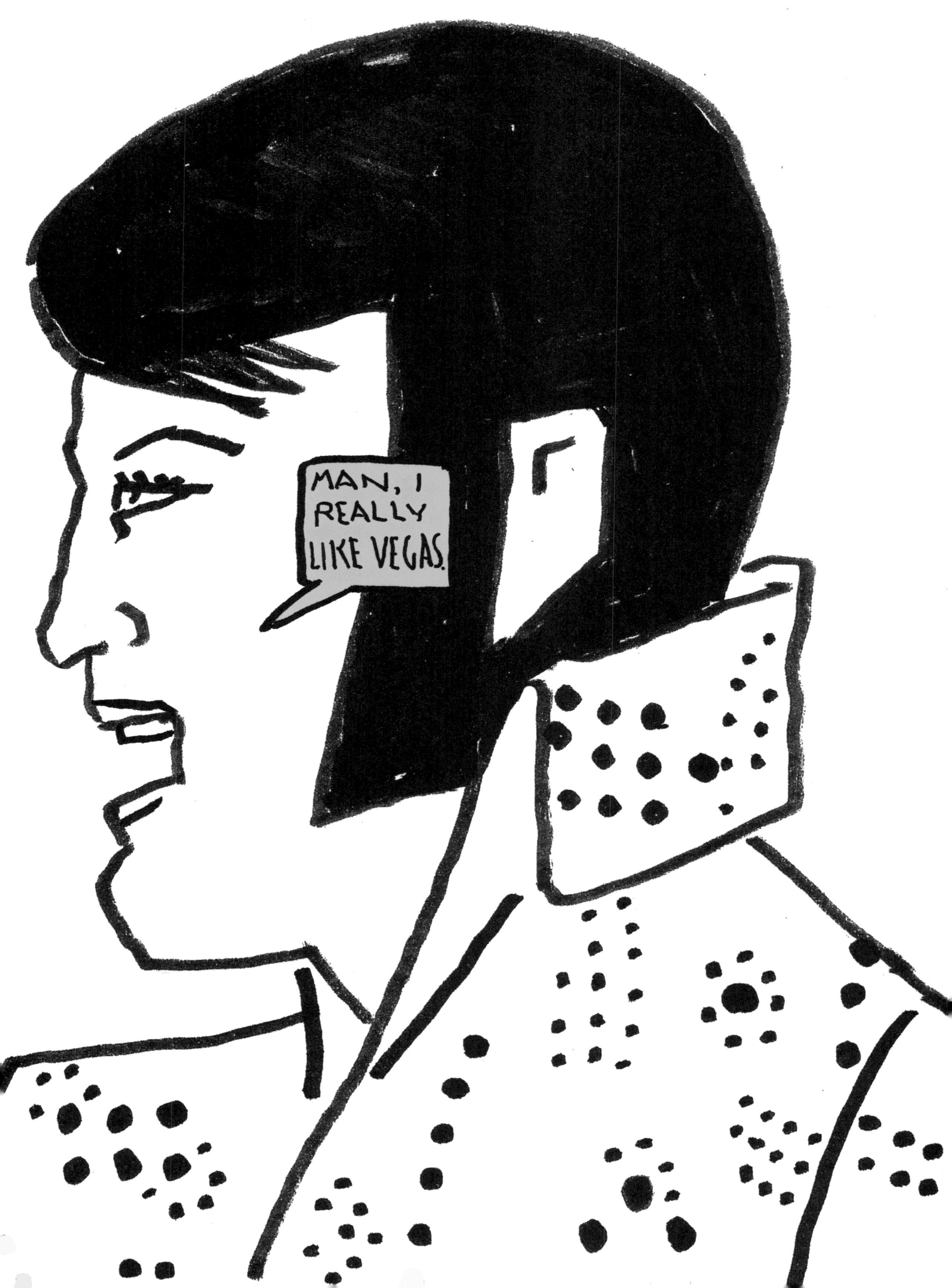
MAN, I REALLY LIKE VEGAS.

What He Ate:

Elvis Presley's Fried Peanut Butter and Banana Sandwich

Total: 10 minutes
Prep: 5 min
Cook: 5 min
Yield: 1 sandwich
Level: Easy

Ingredients
2 slices white bread
2 tablespoons butter
1 small ripe banana
2 tablespoons creamy peanut butter

Place 2 pieces of white bread in the toaster on a light setting. Heat skillet over medium heat with 2 tablespoons butter. While the bread is toasting, in a small bowl, using a fork, mash the ripe banana until it reaches a smooth consistency. Using a knife, take both pieces of the toasted bread and spread 2 tablespoons of creamy peanut butter, topping 1 side with the mashed banana. Place 1 slice of bread on top of the other forming a sandwich. Place sandwich in hot skillet browning each side, flipping with a spatula, about 2 minutes per side. Take out of skillet, slice on a diagonal and serve on a plate.

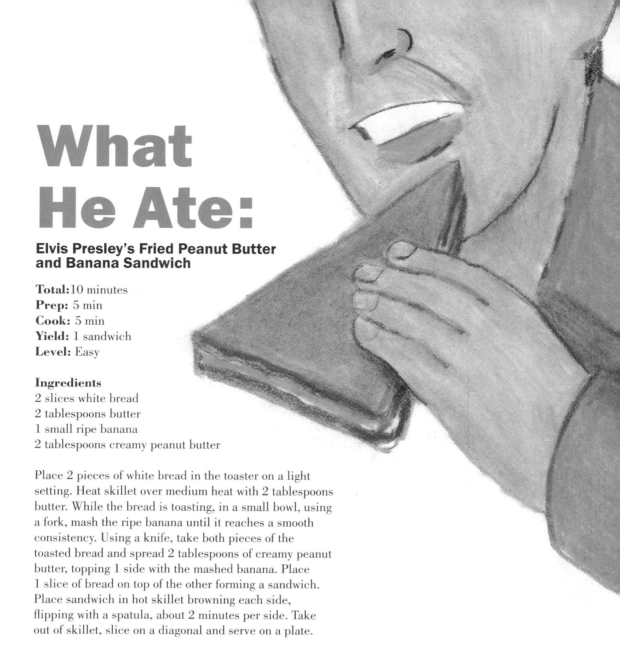

BIBLIOGRAPHY

Burk, Bill E., Early Elvis: The Tupelo Years, Propwash Pub, 1994

Crisafulli, Chris, and Schilling, Jerry, Me and a Guy Named Elvis: My Lifelong Friendship with Elvis Presley, Avery, 2007

dialbforblog.com/archives/85

Dunleavy, Steve, Elvis: What Happened?, Ballantine Books, 1977

elvis.com

elvis.com.au/presley/johnny-cash-remembers-elvis-presley.shtml

elvis-history-blog.com

entertainment.howstuffworks.com/elvis-presley-biography3.htm

graceland.com/blog/elvis-presleys-guitars/

Guralnick, Peter, Last Train to Memphis: The Rise of Elvis Presley, Back Bay Books, 1995

houstonpress.com/music/elvis-30-famous-quotes-about-the-king

Nash, Alanna, The Colonel : The Extraordinary Story of Colonel Tom Parker and Elvis Presley, Aurum Press, 2004

Marcus, Greil, Mystery Train: Images of America in Rock 'n' Roll Music, Plume; Revised edition, 2015

performingsongwriter.com/elvis-presley-love-me-tender

priscilla.elvispresley.com.au

rollingstone.com/music/news/elvis-presley-on-tv-10-unforgettable-broadcasts

thedrive.com/a-list/1586/elvis-couldnt-stop-giving-away-cadillacs

ultimateclassicrock.com/beatles-meet-elvis-presley

uselessinformation.org/early-criticism-elvis-presley

whosdatedwho.com/dating/elvis-presley